ACCLAIM FOR
THE LAST VICTIM

"Few serial killer books have been quite as successful as Jason Moss's."

—*Salon*

"A first-rate, if sobering, true-life drama. It will make anyone who has ever thought about trying to get inside a serial killer's mind think twice."

—**Dennis McDougal, author of the Edgar Award-winning *In the Best of Families* and *Angel of Darkness***

"A tour de force."

—*Las Vegas Sun*

"Informative, insightful, and tough to put down."

—*Syracuse Herald–American*

"A perilous odyssey into the darkest recesses of the psychopathic mind. In this gripping account of his experiences, Moss dares to explore a question that most of us are too terrified to confront: Why are we fascinated to the point of obsession by monsters like John Wayne Gacy and Jeffrey Dahmer? What fearful grip do they exert on us?"

—**Harold Schechter, author of *Human Monsters***

"Spine-tingling . . . fascinates and horrifies . . . a good book."

—*Southern Pines Pilot* (NC)

more . . .

THE LAST VICTIM

THE LAST VICTIM

A True-Life Journey into the Mind of the Serial Killer

JASON MOSS

WITH JEFFREY KOTTLER, Ph.D.

WARNER
VISION
BOOKS

A Time Warner Company

WARNER BOOKS EDITION

Cover design by Diane Luger and Flag
Cover art by Stanislaw Fernandes

Warner Vision is a registered trademark of Warner Books, Inc.

Warner Books, Inc.
1271 Avenue of the Americas
New York, NY 10020

Visit our Web site at
www.twbookmark.com

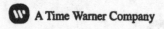 A Time Warner Company

Originally published in hardcover by Warner Books.

ISBN 978-0-446-60827-5

Contents

Prologue
by Jeffrey Kottler,
Ph.D.

It was autumn in the desert, but not like the kind of autumn you'd ordinarily envision for that time of year. It was still hot, blazing hot. The only refuge from the sun was inside the refrigerated buildings.

With its stately palm trees and expanses of grass, the campus resembled one of the many resorts on the Las Vegas Strip. The difference was that, instead of neon and slot machines, there was a hotel college that taught would-be entrepreneurs how to operate casinos, as well as the usual academic buildings that catered mostly to local students and a few Southern California refugees. The most prominent structure by far was the Thomas and Mack Building, the basketball arena that played host to the Runnin' Rebels. This was a university, after all, known primarily for its basketball program.

The best and the brightest of the students, a few hundred ambitious, sometimes compulsive scholars, enrolled in the honors program to get the best shot they could for entrance into medical school, law school, or the corporate fast track. The requirements included several exploratory seminars designed to expand students' education beyond their narrow areas of specialty.

I had volunteered to teach one of these honors seminars, called "Things That Matter." I'd billed it as an opportunity for advanced students to explore a series of topics, including relationships, love, friendship, and, most vitally, the future. And on the first day of class, I encountered an ambitious group of young people: future lawyers, doctors, politicians, CEOs, and scientists.

One student caught my attention immediately because of the way he was dressed. While his peers, aged twenty to twenty-five, wore the uniforms of their generation—jeans, T-shirts, sandals, shorts, even a skateboard or two—this particular student looked as if he'd lost his way en route to a job interview. Beyond his crisp white shirt, striped tie, and polished loafers, I noted a resemblance to one of the Baldwin brothers, William maybe or Alec. He displayed the chiseled good looks that immediately attract the attention of the opposite sex. His eyes were serious, intent, and I noticed he was watching me carefully.

As the semester progressed, this young man stood out for a number of other reasons. He was predictably bright and precocious, even by the standards of an honors program. Yet he was also exceedingly confident and poised. In the jargon of my profession, "he appeared older than his stated age." This was not just because of the way he looked but the way he acted.

"Dr. Kottler," he said one day, addressing me formally even though I preferred the use of my first name, "what exactly is the reason for requiring that our papers describe interviews the way you suggest?"

"Excuse me?" I wasn't sure what he was driving at.

"I mean, if your intent is to get us to reflect on what we learned during this field study, wouldn't it make sense for us to use direct quotes rather than just descriptions of what people said?"

I heard a few classmates snicker. Was he challenging me? "Your point is well taken," I said finally. "I'm looking for a balance between what you observed and the sense you make of those experiences."

As he nodded, I saw looks of admiration from his classmates. Everyone else had been so timid about speaking up, but Jason just jumped in, treating me as a colleague.

My first impression was that he might be a difficult student. Indeed, his eager-to-please attitude toward me—and combative, competitive tone with peers—did create a certain degree of turbulence. Yet in spite of these challenges, I found Jason to be unusually smart, inquisitive, ambitious, and outspoken—and not afraid to advance opinions that might be unusual or unpopular. His style, though provocative and at times trying, actually proved a catalyst for drawing out other students who were quite timid.

The semester-long seminar progressed nicely, perhaps one of my favorites in terms of depth and breadth of issues explored. The only thing that bothered me was the extent to which this group of students was concerned—make that *obsessed*—with achievement. So many of their questions revolved around how various actions would affect their final grades.

In a class of hard chargers, Jason stood out as especially intense. He found reasons to approach me after many classes, wanting very specific directions about future assignments. While at first I was annoyed by these overtures, which seemed transparently driven toward getting an *A*, I soon recognized that Jason was reaching out for help.

It became our pattern to escort one another to our next classes. During these strolls across campus, Jason confided in me about his plans for the future, conflicts with his family, and the relationship with his girlfriend. In everything he talked about, and everything he did, he struck me as incredibly driven. I urged him to lighten up a bit, to stop trying so hard to do everything perfectly. Perhaps I recognized more than a little of myself in him. I too was an avid approval seeker who found it difficult to slow down.

I noticed that in spite of all that Jason had accomplished thus far in life, as an athlete, a scholar, and personality on campus, he didn't seem to be having much fun. Actually, he seemed haunted.

He was a straight-*A* student, chief justice of the student government, president of the psychology honors society, and a leader in community civic organizations. As we walked around campus, students, faculty, even administrators whom I barely knew by sight seemed familiar with him.

At times he would press me for advice about personal matters, and each time I'd deftly put the focus back on him, as a counseling professor can easily do. I'll admit to feeling flattered he was willing to trust me: I could tell it was difficult for him to open up.

As the semester wound down, Jason and I got together for our last meeting. He thanked me for a stimulating class, then caught me by surprise by abruptly changing the subject. Shyly, he invited me to attend his honors thesis presentation.

I reluctantly agreed. These presentations, which were

usually about some obscure area of research I could barely follow, could be quite boring. In fact, I couldn't help grimacing as I reflected on the last one I'd attended. Dealing with political corruption in East Africa, it might have been interesting if there hadn't been so much sparring among the faculty committee members, each of whom was eager to demonstrate his expertise.

As the day for the event approached, I felt a little better about going. I didn't really have the time, but it was a constructive ritual and I felt honored that Jason thought enough of me to extend an invitation. Usually there are only a handful of people in attendance—three faculty members on the student's committee and perhaps a friend or a parent.

I was shocked, therefore, when I walked into the room—make that *the auditorium*—and found seventy or eighty people. Somehow, word had gotten out that something unusual was going to happen. I had no idea that the next few hours would hold me spellbound, propelling me through emotions that ranged from indignation to admiration.

Jason stood before the audience in his new suit, anxiously pacing as he waited for the signal to begin. I could hear the crowd buzzing with anticipation, although I couldn't quite make out what they were saying. "Can you believe it!" "Jason . . . gotta be a little . . . I sure wouldn't . . ." "So I was—" "Shsssh! He's starting!"

"In this presentation," Jason began nervously, "I will be talking about accessing the minds of various serial killers from the perspective of their victims." You could hear a collective gasp from the audience. Then complete silence, as if we were all holding our breath to see what would come next.

"Although much is known about the patterns of their behavior," Jason continued, "even the nature of their child-hoods, their motives and fantasies, we really know very little about how they manage to overpower people, manipulate and degrade them, get them to do things they wouldn't otherwise consider."

He then went on to relate how, while only a freshman in college, he'd figured out a way to lure a half dozen of the most notorious serial killers into communication with him, eventually forging full-blown relationships with several. In each case, he researched meticulously what would interest them the most and then cast himself in the role of disciple, admirer, businessman, surrogate, or potential victim. In a few instances, he actually interviewed the killers in prison, winning their trust and uncovering their secrets. Perhaps even more remarkable, in one case he was able to experience, firsthand, what it's like to be stalked, seduced, manipulated, and eventually trapped by a deranged murderer who'd killed more than thirty times previously.

If Jason's overview wasn't chilling enough, it was downright eerie to hear recordings of the killers' voices and see samples of their perverted writing.

As I watched and listened to what Jason had done, I was flooded with questions. While everyone else in the room seemed captivated by the tales of perversion and mayhem committed by killers Jason had contacted, I was curious about what would motivate an eighteen-year-old to undertake a project like this, one that would not only jeopardize his sanity but his physical safety. Little did I realize at the time that I'd be the one entrusted with the task of helping Jason tell his story.

When I met with him a few days later he wanted to know if I'd be interested in collaborating with him on a book an-

alyzing the motives and behavior of his most ardent corre-
spondent, John Wayne Gacy. In Illinois during the 1970s,
Gacy kidnapped, tortured, raped, and killed at least thirty-
three young boys and buried many of them in his basement.

"Jason," I addressed him solemnly, "I'm really flattered
that you'd ask for my help with this."

He looked away from me, preparing himself for what he
anticipated would be rejection.

"I really *am* intrigued with what you've done," I reassured him. "It's just . . ."

"You don't understand," he interrupted. "Nobody really
understands. . . ."

I put my hand on his shoulder to stop what I could see
was the beginning of an argument. It's not a good idea to
get Jason started unless you're prepared for a very long discussion, and I had other students waiting.

"You misunderstand me," I told him. "Please, just listen.
Let me finish."

He nodded his head, but I could see his impatience. By
now he'd grown used to people not "getting" his peculiar
area of fascination.

I decided to be blunt. "Jason, nobody cares about Gacy
anymore. The guy died, what, four years ago? There's another one to take his place, somebody new the public wants
to know about."

"Yeah," he jumped in again, "but Gacy was special.
There's been nobody like him. And besides, this book
wouldn't just be about Gacy. Remember, I also communicated with Charles Manson and Jeffrey Dahmer and
Richard Ramirez, and—"

"I realize that, Jason," I quickly interjected. "It's just that books have been written about Gacy and these other guys before—"

"So?" he interrupted. "What are you saying? That I shouldn't do this? That all this work I put into—"

"No, quite the contrary. What I'm saying is that the book shouldn't be exclusively about these serial killers but also about *you*. People would want to know why an eighteen-year-old kid contacted Gacy and the others in the first place. They'd be curious what would drive someone so young to want to study and control them. You have to admit, that's not the usual hobby for someone just out of high school."

I laughed as I said this—until I noticed Jason's pained expression. He was used to being seen as a bit different from others his age.

"In order to understand your motives and what drives you," I continued, "we'd have to start from the beginning."

"I already did that in the thesis. I started with the first letter I wrote to Gacy."

"No, I mean from the *very* beginning. People will want to know about your family and background. How you got into this sort of stuff. How you managed to convince your parents to let you do this, how you hid other things from them. In some ways, this story is too incredible to believe. We'd have to lay the foundation."

Indeed, the first thing I did was corroborate everything I could related to Jason's thesis. I conducted interviews with Jason's parents, separately and together, comparing their versions of the same events. I talked with his brother and friends. I spoke with other faculty who knew Jason. I looked through the hundreds of letters he'd received from various killers, following them sequentially. I listened to

tapes of conversations he'd had with Gacy. At one point I
even traveled with him on one of his research excursions to
Death Row.

Once I was able to confirm and document the *details* of
Jason's story, I investigated the *context* of what occurred.
Slowly, a more complete picture of this young man began
to take shape. He was obviously a precocious, talented kid,
mature beyond his years. His parents, both working-class
and down-to-earth, had no idea what to do with a son who
constantly challenged and mystified them. Since they
couldn't seem to control their child's behavior, and since he
had never, ever gotten in trouble or, in an academic setting,
performed in less than exemplary fashion, they found it
easy to give in to him. When they did try to rein him in, he
still found ways around them.

Although blessed with high intelligence and formidable
verbal and athletic skills, Jason was vulnerable and inse-
cure. He received a number of paradoxical messages growing up: at the same time that he was insulated from graphic
violence and forbidden to see horror films, his mother was
a true-crime aficionado who left lurid books lying around
the house. He found his parents' behavior volatile and unpredictable. He learned to be a chameleon as a way to protect himself, changing forms according to others' moods.
He honed his talent for pleasing others to a fine art, reading
perceptively what others most desire and then presenting
himself in ways designed to win trust.

A natural mimic and fearless risk taker, Jason studied
psychology systematically, hoping to land a job someday as
a famous prosecutor or FBI agent. Nobody who knew him
scoffed at what he might be capable of accomplishing: this
was a kid who was going places. Certainly, nobody had

more determination and ambition. The one discordant note was that his very existence depended so much on being seen as special and unique.

In the story that follows—written in Jason's own words with my assistance—you'll meet Jason as he first stumbles onto his project's central feature: that it might be possible for a teenager like himself to pull off what law enforcement and psychiatric experts have tried, and largely failed, to do—learn the homicidal tactics and secret fantasies of men who've killed twenty, thirty, even hundreds of times in the most grisly fashion imaginable. You'll learn about the early childhood experiences that propelled Jason toward his bizarre hobby. You'll see the reasons for his exaggerated self-importance, understand why cockiness occasionally creeps into his voice as he talks about his triumphs over these celebrity killers. Jason wanted so badly to be recognized and validated. He wanted to feel powerful. And what better way to do so than to deceive and control the world's most famous human predators?

Jason's personal motives aside, I believe that this story is unique in the annals of true-crime literature. By peering over Jason's shoulder, we're able to catch a glimpse at "the point of transaction," the exact moment when a serial killer makes contact with his victim and begins to reel him in. We're able to witness, through Jason's senses, exactly what it looks and sounds like, what it *feels* like, to be manipulated, controlled, and dominated by a serial killer.

Yet this narrative is not just one precocious kid's tale of a bizarre dance with the devil—or, rather, several devils. In a broader sense, it's a portrait of the choreographed interactions between killers and victims everywhere. It describes, in excruciating detail, exactly how someone, even a person who is unusually vigilant, cautious, and intentional, can be drawn into the web of a killer who essentially makes a living stalking others.

Looked at one way, this is an adventure story in which a David attempts to take on a whole herd of Goliaths. Yet it is also an immensely disturbing narrative, sexually explicit, perverse, and filled with brutality; it requires a strong stomach.

One can't help but ask what would lead a person, especially someone so young, to enter this world willingly. Why would a first-year college student spend his time researching ways to ingratiate himself with murderers? Why would he risk using himself as bait?

The truth is that many of us are fascinated with murder, killing, and violence. The whole genre of true-crime books testifies to that, as does the popularity of films and novels in which graphic murder plays a central role. Jason's actions are thus emblematic of a culture in which violence is entertainment and murderers have become celebrities. Every new killer on the scene attracts his own share of groupies, fans, or spectators who can't get enough details about the grisly crimes. Web pages are devoted exclusively to following the exploits of famous killers, analyzing the grisly details of their crimes. Ironically, the biggest challenge Jason faced when he embarked on this project was how to capture the interest of someone like Charles Manson or John Wayne Gacy, given that they enjoyed the attention of thousands of fans who wrote weekly, sending them gifts and vying for their attention.

Before committing to this project I first had to wrestle with certain ethical issues. As a therapist, and trainer of other therapists, among the most important values to me are authenticity and honesty, being completely open and straight with people. But here is a story in which a person resorts to deceit and manipulation to learn information that can't be gained any other way. While I was impressed by all the things Jason learned, his modus operandi seemed fraught with moral conundrums.

In the end I believed this was an important story to tell, not only because of what it uncovers about homicidal relationships, but also what it reveals about our culture that so glorifies violence and turns killers into celebrities. If Jason's experiences tell us anything, it is that pretending affinity with perpetrators of evil will, over time, wreak dire consequences on the psyche.

When Jason embarked on his quest, he was too young to realize what a professional might have told him: that, having stepped into the devil's lair, it's sometimes impossible to leave the nightmares behind. In a very real sense, Jason Moss was—for John Wayne Gacy, Richard Ramirez, Henry Lee Lucas, Jeffrey Dahmer, and Charles Manson—their last victim.

THE LAST
VICTIM

1

The Bookstore

There's a little strip mall in an older, residential area in Las Vegas, far from the chaos of the other, more famous Strip. From the university, it's a straight shot down Flamingo Road, a major artery of the city named after Bugsy Siegel's original resort.

Typical of such malls, the row of shops contains an insurance agency, a hobby shop, an army recruiting office, a tuxedo rental outlet, a beauty shop, a used bookstore, and the obligatory Chinese restaurant with a $4.75 lunch special. There's also a kickboxing studio, which is why on this particular day in August 1993 I happened to be there.

I was early for my appointment with my karate instructor and I needed a place to escape the heat. Assessing my options, the bookstore seemed especially inviting—cool and quiet inside, and with plenty to occupy my attention. I was already feeling a bit stressed from my first week as a university student, so I welcomed a few minutes to literally chill out.

As I began strolling the aisles, I noticed I was one of the store's few customers. Even so, I was invisible to the bored cashier, who was alternately thumbing through a book and taking inventory of others lying on the counter. In fact, there were books *everywhere*, some still resting in boxes, others neatly organized on the shelves. It was as if the owner couldn't quite figure out how to make inflow and outflow mesh.

Because true crime had been an interest of mine since my early teens, I soon found myself in the store's crime section, staring at titles that somehow seemed familiar: *Killer Cults, FBI Killer, Evil Harvest, Brother in Blood*. I couldn't help noticing that, more often than not, "blood" was the common denominator: *Blood Echoes, Blood Games, Blood Lust, Blood Sister, Blood Warning*. Whoever came up with these titles seemed to have a thing for blood.

Like many people, I was secretly—and a bit guiltily— fascinated by such material. It can be exciting to peek through your fingers at something forbidden and terrible. Just ask the millions of rubberneckers who slow down at accident scenes, hoping to catch a glimpse of a body.

Among the hundreds of books that screamed with promises of blood and pain, one in particular caught my interest: *Hunting Humans*. A big, thick encyclopedic volume, it presented profiles of some of the world's most famous serial killers. As I stood in the narrow aisle turning pages, I began reflecting on how well camouflaged these predators are, prior to being caught. They look like anyone else, live apparently normal lives, often appear charming, sociable, and productive. But at the same time, they stalk and kill people, sometimes torturing and mutilating them.

I wondered what it must be like to look in the mirror

and realize *you* are the bogeyman. *How are these people able to live with themselves?*

I was jolted out of my reverie by the sound of voices coming from across the aisle. "Do you have a store credit?" I could hear the cashier ask someone. I didn't catch the answer because, in my mind, an idea was beginning to form. It was something on the edge of my consciousness—something I couldn't grab on to.

The title of another book captured my attention: *The Killer Clown.* Now, *that's* interesting, I thought, reaching for it. I'd always been afraid of clowns.

As a child my most frequent nightmare took place at my grandparents' house. In the dream I was supposed to be taking a bath, but a strange sound drew me out of the tub to investigate. I started walking toward the stairs when I heard a scream, followed by a liquidy cackle. Looking down the stairs, I saw my grandmother sprawled out on the floor, blood slowly dripping from her mouth. Somewhere close, I heard an eerie laughter.

I turned in the direction of the voice and was startled to see a clown sitting on the stairwell's balcony, laughing at me. I particularly remember the big red smile on his face. At that point, I'd always wake up.

My parents and grandparents tell me that, as a kid, whenever I'd see a clown, I'd start crying in fear. Even today, there's something about that painted-on happy face and exaggerated show of good cheer that I don't trust. There's something about the masks that clowns wear—I can't help feeling that the intention is to *deceive.* Call me paranoid, but I find myself wondering: Who's the *real* person hiding beneath that makeup?

The idea that a killer would dress himself up as a clown

to entertain sick children by day, and then stalk the streets for prey at night, seemed inconceivable to me. Yet I *could* identify with people who led double lives. How many times had I exuded confidence when taking an exam, or engaging in a debate, when, in fact, I was less than sure of myself?

I decided to buy both books—the one about hunting humans, and the other about the killer clown—even though it would put a crimp in my student budget. At the time, I had no idea the true cost would ultimately be much higher.

2

True Crime

On the drive home from the kickboxing session, I glanced over at the passenger seat and saw my new purchases lying on top of my backpack. Clearly, I was enthralled by these types of books, and yet I felt very ambivalent about it, since true crime is also an interest of my mother's. We fought a lot, my mother and I—usually about her wanting to control my life in some way. I tried to distance myself from her as much as I could, and it really bothered me that we now shared this interest.

My mother couldn't get enough of "slasher" books. Ever since I was little, I'd seen her hunched over them, shaking her head at their grisly contents. As far back as I can remember, our kitchen table was stacked with books featuring lurid covers and even more graphic photo sections.

Usually, the books were obtained from the public library, a regular destination for my mother and me. I'd get lost in the long, endless aisles while she searched for titles that interested her. Eventually, we'd both end up in the back reading room, which had been designed for toddlers to comb through picture books. I have vivid memories of walls decorated with large pictures of rainbows and oversize happy-faced suns.

In the very back of the room, there was a table close to the wall. Even after I was older—but before I'd reached the age where going to the library with your mom was no longer considered cool—the two of us would sit at that table and talk about our selections.

On one particular day—I was thirteen at the time—she plunked her books on the table and exclaimed, "Jason, you won't believe this one!" She pulled a volume from the middle of her pile and, with an I've-got-a-secret grin on her face, began leafing through the pages.

"What's it about?" I asked apprehensively. I knew what was coming next.

"You'll never believe it. Wait until you hear what this one guy did. It's so disgusting."

So why are you telling me about it? I wondered. Still, I knew better than to challenge her. The library was about to close, so only about half the lights were still on. The muted light lent the room a spooky atmosphere that made me feel even more on edge.

"Aw, Mom, let's get outta here."

"No, not yet," she said. "I want to show you this."

"Come on . . ." I said, rolling my eyes.

"This will just take a few minutes. There's this guy who would take the skin off the women he'd kill and save it. He was trying to make a suit of real human flesh. He wanted to be a woman."

Why couldn't my mother read cookbooks or something? I tried to interrupt, but she was on a roll.

"He kept a whole box of women's vaginas," she said.

"He made a belt of human nipples. He had lamp shades made of human flesh."

Now, although it was certainly my life's ambition to see a real-life vagina, to date I'd never had the pleasure of a viewing, and I had great difficulty imagining a whole box of them. And what on earth did someone do with a belt made of nipples?

"That's great, Mom, but I really think we need to leave. They're closing the place soon. Look, the lights are going out."

"Wait. Just a minute. You have to see this." She opened the book to some glossy pictures.

"Isn't it gross?" she asked me. "The police found it when they entered the killer's house."

My mother pointed to a photo of a female corpse, hanging upside down from a wooden beam. The woman had been decapitated and her body was sliced down the middle from her throat all the way to her vagina. All of her major organs had been removed.

"Jason, you *really* should read this book."

"But you've already told me all the good parts," I deadpanned. She couldn't tell if I was kidding or not.

"Do you want me to check this book out or not?"

"No!" I said adamantly. "I don't want to even *hear* about this sick stuff. And I'm gonna tell Dad about all this crap you're reading."

My mother started looking around, embarrassed by my outburst. We both realized it was time to get out of there. I was so angry I could barely talk. As usual, my mother had no idea what I was so upset about.

Although that day my mother's enthusiasm had rubbed me the wrong way, eventually I *did* become intrigued with the books she was reading. Over the next year, she continued to tell me about crime stories she'd heard or read about. And pretty soon I was reading them, too. Reading them voraciously.

I was amazed by the power these killers wielded—not just their physical power in some cases but their power to stun a nation. I was intrigued by how they could terrify even the most unflappable and cause armies of law enforcement officials to scramble madly in search of them. Even as these predators disgusted me, I envied the public attention they commanded. Too, against my better impulses, I found myself admiring the artful way many of them stalked their prey and eluded detection.

Eventually, as a kind of self-dare—one intended to relieve teenage tedium more than anything—I began pretending to *be* the person I was reading about. I know that sounds weird, but I really wanted to figure out why and how these people could do what they do.

I imagined what it would be like to stalk and kill. I put aside all I'd been taught about right and wrong. I tried to pretend I was someone without a conscience. I tried to get to that level of consciousness where one exults in being truly evil.

It was terrifying to be in that dark, remote place. A place where sanity is experienced as something *outside*. I'm not sure I ever fully got there. I am, after all, a sane person, a moral person. But the attempt to reach "the other side" was exhilarating.

As I shifted in the car seat to work out the stiffness from my kickboxing lesson, I spied my driveway up ahead. The suburban house we lived in was, for that area, pretty much standard issue: red tile roof, white stucco walls. It had been a comfortable place to grow up in, and, as I was already coming to learn, it could be a welcome refuge from the pressures of university life.

As I turned off the engine, I once again glanced at my new books. What sort of house had the Killer Clown grown up in? I wondered. Was it a place from which sanity had fled? A dark place? Or a place much like mine?

3

First Target

Our house had the lived-in look you'd expect, knowing that two teenage boys were in residence. There was enough room for my mother, father, fourteen-year-old brother, and me to each have our own space, but increasingly I felt closed in, and I resented more and more the constant monitoring of my activities. Lately, it seemed like whatever I did drew criticism, especially from my mother.

"Jason," I could hear her yell from out in the garage, just as I'd settled in with one of my books. "I'm back with the groceries—get out here and help me."

"Just a minute," I grunted, frustrated that she was obviously in one of her "moods." It never seemed to take much for us to end up in a fight, but lately, we were butting heads all the time. When the two of us went at it, my brother and father gave us a wide berth.

We all loved each other and, most of the time, supported one another, but I seemed to end up in the middle of any disagreement. My father was really a nice guy, kind and always supportive, but he deferred to my mom a lot, letting her make most of the decisions. Whether by choice or circumstance, she became the disciplinarian—the one who made sure my brother and I did our schoolwork and took care of our chores. She also threw up roadblocks whenever I wanted to do something that deviated from the straight and narrow.

I'm a fighter myself, unwilling to give in without a battle, so we were constantly going at each other while my brother and father stood on the sidelines. It's legend in our family, and maybe it's true, that my mom and I continually get in each other's way because we're so alike. That theory seemed borne out this particular afternoon when she found me reading at the kitchen counter.

"Jason," she said in exasperation, walking into the house with an armload of grocery bags, "I'm not carrying in all these bags by myself. Didn't you *hear* me?"

"Sorry, Mom," I meant to say contritely, but it came out sarcastic. "I was doing something important. Do you expect me to drop everything and come running every time you come home?"

"Yes. And make sure to put the milk in the fridge."

While I was busy unloading the car, my mother discovered what I'd been up to. "Hey, you've got some great books here. When can I read them?"

"You *can't*," I told her, reaching up to put a can on the shelf. "*I'm* reading them now. Besides, you shouldn't read this kind of stuff. You can't handle it." To punctuate the last remark, I slammed the cupboard door.

"You're the one who can't handle blood," she teased. "I hope you don't pass out while you're reading." My mother loved to make fun of me because I had a weak stomach for any sort of blood or gore. Some of the favorite stories in my family were of me fainting.

Ignoring her, I went back to my book about the Killer Clown, John Wayne Gacy.

"Isn't that one about the guy who tortured and killed all those boys and then buried them under his house?" my mom asked, noticing the cover.

"Yeah," I answered, hoping she'd go away.

"Then you'd better leave it alone. You've always been afraid of clowns."

Leave it to my mother to get in the last word. Even *she* couldn't get to me that day, though.

I was fascinated by Gacy's story—it was such a strange tale. Here was this guy making $300,000 a year, in 1970 yet. He's got this successful business. He's head of the Jaycees and volunteers his time to help sick kids. The book even had a picture of him standing next to Rosalyn Carter, wife of the president. Incredible!

Meanwhile, he's torturing his victims for hours, even days, at a time.

I read about one unlucky guy, about *my* age, who was picked up at a bus station while he was waiting for his scheduled departure. Gacy brought the guy home and then raped him repeatedly before he began torturing him, playing Russian roulette with a loaded pistol and then submerging his face in a bathtub full of water to the point where he passed out. Then he violated the kid again with various objects around the house, all the while screaming at him that he was going to die.

The more I read, the queasier I started to feel, and yet I couldn't put the book down. Gacy's victims were the same age I was. They even *resembled* me physically. I couldn't help but wonder what I would have done if he'd tried to capture *me*. I may have been a weight lifter and kickboxer, but it was clear that each of these strong, athletic guys Gacy preyed upon was somehow tricked into submission. I thought to myself, I'd just love to see Gacy try that stuff on me. Well, maybe not.

It was at that moment that the vague idea that had tugged at the edge of my consciousness in the bookstore began to clarify itself. I wondered what would happen if I wrote Gacy a letter. I read that he was still on Death Row waiting for his scheduled execution. I figured he was probably pretty bored and in need of diversion.

For me, the question wasn't why I'd write someone like Gacy, but why anyone wouldn't be curious about what made him the way he was. Was the act of killing for the thirty-third time any different from the seventeenth? How could this guy excel at maintaining two separate lives—community leader by day and murderous predator by night? It seemed to me that these were questions anyone would want answered.

The more I read about serial killers, the more convinced I became that the so-called experts—the police and forensic psychologists—weren't exploring all possible avenues of inquiry. Surely, what was needed was more than having captured killers fill out questionnaires and submit to interviews. I wondered what kind of effort had been made to debrief the *victims*—those who'd lived to tell the tale.

In a burst of inspiration, I considered what I might learn if I approached someone like Gacy in the guise of one of his victims.

Of course, most kids my age—or adults, for that matter—would never even think about taking on a project like this. But I'd done some pretty crazy things in the past, and, to tell you the truth, I needed to divert myself with something that wasn't school-related. After going to college for a week, I could tell that, in many ways, it was going to be an extension of high school. I was living at home, and I desperately wanted some excitement in my life. Further, I hoped for a job in law enforcement someday, maybe even one with the FBI. For that dream to happen, I knew I'd have to distinguish myself in some way.

If gaining the trust of a serial killer didn't get the Bureau's attention, what would?

The Plan

At dinner a few nights later I decided to float my idea. My father and mother were talking about work, as usual. My dad works as a salesperson in a department store, my mom as a cashier in one of the local casinos. Both are usually tired at the end of the day after dealing with demanding people. Still, they make the effort to schedule a family meal each night.

My younger brother, Jarrod, was eyeballing me while our parents yakked. I smiled and made a funny face to entertain him. I was waiting for a break in the conversation.

"Hey, wait until you hear my latest idea," I finally said, interrupting my parents' chatter.

"Mom, can I have some more spaghetti?" my brother asked.

"Jarrod, I'm *talking*," I said, giving him a look. After a moment of silence and an intake of breath, I began: "I'm going to write a letter to John Wayne Gacy, maybe even to Jeffrey Dahmer or Charles Manson."

My brother choked on the bread. My parents just sat there, saying nothing.

"Did you guys hear what I said? I've been reading about these serial killers. Several of them are still alive. They're on Death Row, waiting to be executed."

I could see my mother roll her eyes. She got up from the table to get more pasta and sauce. My brother and I could really put away the food.

"Dad, did you hear me?" I looked directly at him. "Don't you think that would be cool? What if they wrote back? That would be awesome. Don't you think?"

"Sure, I guess," he answered noncommittally, and buried himself in the pasta.

"Why on earth would you want to write a killer?" my mother asked. "And why would he write back to some kid like you? You're not even allowed to do something like that."

"Where'd you get *that* idea?" I challenged her. "I can write whomever I choose."

My brother came to my defense. "Yeah, where do you get that from?"

"Look," I said, "it's no big deal. I know it's sort of outrageous, but that's why it's so cool. Who else would do this? Besides, these guys are all locked away in prison. What's the harm?"

Jarrod started giggling. "What if they write you letters in blood?"

Then my dad got into the act as well. "What if they ask for a pint of your blood?" Now all three of them were laughing.

"Can't you guys ever be serious?" I complained. "Just imagine a letter from Charles Manson coming to the house. That would be so freaky."

"There'll be no letters from killers coming to *this* house!" declared my mother.

My dad jumped in. "Calm down, Sue. What's the big deal? Let him write the letters. Nobody's going to write him back."

"Don't tell *me* to calm down!" she huffed. "This is my house and Jason isn't going to do whatever the hell he wants. It'll be like all the other stuff you let him do—we'll end up suffering for it. There'll be no letters coming to this house!"

I was about to take the argument to the next level when my father kicked me under the table. "Just relax, Sue," he reassured my mother. "Nobody's going to write any letters. Let's just enjoy the dinner."

"Well, if I *were* to write a letter," I added, now talking directly to my father, "you know I'd have to use our return address. I've been thinking about this. If I used a post office box, someone like Gacy would know immediately that I have something to hide."

"But you *do* have something to hide," my mother pointed out—more calmly this time. "You're just a young—"

"Mom, Dad, I know what I'm doing," I interrupted. "I really do. You've got to trust me on this."

"So why don't you use someone else's address?" my father countered, partly to appease my mother.

"Because if I use another address, he might check. Gacy, for example, had a lot of friends before he was captured. He used to live here in Las Vegas. He could send one of them over just to make sure I am who I say I am."

"That's exactly my point," said my mother. "I won't

have any friends of these killers coming to my house. I simply won't tolerate it!"

I knew it was senseless to continue the discussion any further. I could work on my dad later and then he'd convince my mother to ease up. The killers probably wouldn't write back anyway, so what was the difference?

Later that night, my thoughts returned to my embryonic project. After reviewing my list of potential serial killer "pen pals," I confirmed my initial intuition that John Wayne Gacy was the most intriguing. He seemed to be the embodiment of all evil, the living example of everything I feared most. Unlike some of the others, he was totally invisible when he was operating. There was no way you could tell what he was up to. He wasn't a crazed lunatic like Manson or a loner like Dahmer; rather, he projected the appearance of a normal guy whom most anyone would like.

I had to talk to someone about my plan, but it was clear my parents had already heard as much as they cared to. As an alternative, I thought I might try bouncing a few ideas off of my girlfriend, Jennifer.

I'd met Jenn in high school, where I'd always see her in the hallway on my way to English class. She was so stunningly beautiful that just a glance from her would make me speechless. She had long black glistening hair and these gorgeous big brown eyes that contrasted with her smooth, soft skin. Finally, one day I worked up the nerve to introduce myself and we'd dated continuously ever since.

Jennifer added balance to my life. I was critical and mistrustful of people; she always saw the best in them. I was ambitious and future-oriented; she lived in the present, unconcerned with what would happen tomorrow. I tended to be serious; she was a free spirit, always ready to laugh and play. Naturally, there was some tension between us, given our different personalities and values, but we were both grateful for the ways we brought out the best in each other.

Jenn came from a strict Cuban family, devoutly Catholic. Religious paraphernalia could be found all over the walls of their home. Though it didn't occur to me at the time, because of their religious outlook, Jenn and her mother, Teresa, were probably not the most receptive audience for my "exciting idea."

"You're going to write who?" they both asked, incredulous.

I explained a little about what I'd been up to, the books I'd bought, how I'd gotten the idea to try to persuade a number of serial killers to correspond with me by pretending to be someone they'd find appealing. Then I explained how I settled on Gacy as my first target.

"*Dios mío!*" Teresa blurted out. "Who in their right mind would do such a thing as try to make friends with a killer?"

She then turned to Jenn and began talking rapidly in Spanish. All I could make out were the words "*Tu novio está loco.*"

Before I could say anything, Teresa was in my face again: "Don't let my husband find out or he'll throw you right out of this house."

I was Jenn's first boyfriend, and although her parents tried to accept me, they found me a bit weird, even for an Anglo. They didn't like the idea that I was a fan of horror movies, or that I'd once written a paper on witchcraft. Jenn was on the defensive most of the time, and I loved her for sticking up for me.

"Enough, Mama!" Jenn put in. "Daddy isn't going to throw Jason out." She then turned to me. "But seriously, how come you never mentioned this idea to me before?" She seemed to be more upset that I might have been hiding something from her, rather than by what I was proposing to do.

"I've just been thinking about it for a few days. You know how much I'm into this stuff," I said, shrugging. It was a point of tension in our relationship that I liked going to horror movies and she didn't.

Jenn cringed. It was obvious I'd embarrassed her in front of her mother. She was almost pleading when she said, "Why can't I have a normal boyfriend?"

Teresa nodded her head and crossed herself. "Do your parents know about this? Your parents would never go for this. Chica, look, he's smiling! *Es una broma.* Why do you play around for?"

"I'm not joking. Someone needs to study and find out about these people. I—"

"What makes you think you can talk to these people?" Teresa interrupted. "You're asking for trouble."

I decided to shut up before things *really* got heated. This discussion hadn't gone the way I'd expected it to.

As Teresa fled upstairs muttering to herself, I looked at Jenn, hoping for support.

"Jason," she said, sighing, "you're not normal. Sometimes the things you say to me, the ideas you have—they're just so . . . I don't know . . . strange. Someday I'm going to be on a talk show titled 'My Boyfriend Writes to Serial Killers.'"

She said that with a smile, so I figured we'd be okay.

5

Research

It was pretty clear to me at this point that I couldn't talk frankly to anyone about what I was doing. When I looked at myself through the eyes of my family or friends, I really *did* seem strange. Wherever I was going, I was going alone.

Rather than fear the prospect of single-handedly taking on someone like Gacy, though, I felt a measure of pride that I was willing to attempt something nobody else would. Naively, I believed I could outthink and outmanipulate Gacy and the other predators I intended to write. In my fantasies, they became *my* victims as I accessed all the valuable things they were keeping from law enforcement and mental health experts.

Though at the time I lacked the self-awareness to see it, I was definitely suffering from delusions of grandeur.

As I thought more about it, I decided the best way to attract Gacy's attention, given the killer's homosexuality, was to pretend to be sexually confused and highly impressionable. I would concoct some stories about my childhood that mirrored his own childhood—for example, I'd claim that

I'd been sexually abused when I was younger and that my father had bullied me.

One obvious problem was that I understood so little about the world Gacy inhabited. I was going to pretend to be gay, or at least leaning in that direction, and I didn't know the first thing about what that meant.

I've always been curious about things that are beyond my own experience—especially if they're the least bit forbidden. I remember one time Jenn and I passed a cemetery—a very unusual-looking one—and on a whim, I pretended to be shopping for a plot so as to get a tour of the place. I've followed this same pattern again and again, whenever I've seen something that appeals to me, or scares me.

The whole world of homosexuality was, to me, foreign, but also, as a culture, fascinating. I'd had gay acquaintances in the past and I admired the courage it took to deal with the stuff they had to face on a daily basis. Like most other kids my age, I feared such a lifestyle, felt threatened by it—did one choose it, or did it choose you? And up to that point, I'd never had the courage to ask any direct questions. Nevertheless, I knew that if I was serious about "getting over" on the likes of John Gacy and Jeffrey Dahmer, I would have to know a lot more about the worlds they inhabited.

One idea I had was to talk to a male prostitute so I could at least learn the appropriate jargon and customs. As it happened, I'd already road-tested this strategy on a female prostitute sometime before. It was a typical "Jason experience." I happened to be walking down the Strip with some friends when she approached us. Most suburban teenage boys would, of course, have muttered a sheepish "No thanks" and skittered away. But with an audience of my peers to perform for, I did exactly the opposite. I pretended to be an interested customer long enough to get her life story, and she even ended up buying us dinner.

I decided to start my research by asking the bartender in a local gay bar for some direction. I was prepared to feel uncomfortable, and, in fact, the whole scene was a bit disorienting. As I stood at the bar talking to the bartender, I noticed some of the patrons checking me out. I suppose it was flattering, but all I could feel was relief that I felt no inclination to respond to their interest.

The bartender advised me to check out the personal ads in a particular newspaper. I looked through the possibilities available and settled on one of them: "For all night companionship, call Rico. Experienced pleasure."

I called Rico on the phone that very night, half persuaded that I'd pushed the envelope too far this time. I was afraid he might get the wrong idea, that he'd think I wanted more than to talk.

"Hello," he answered on the second ring.

"Hi, is this Rico?" I said, not at all acting in my role as the nervous patron. "I saw your ad."

"So," he replied in a seductive voice, "what can I do for you?"

"I was wondering if we could meet somewhere, so we could talk."

"Good, because I don't like to talk over the phone. Why don't we meet at the bowling alley at Sam's Town Casino?"

"That sounds fine. Let's say, an hour."

I still had time to back out of this meeting. What if someone I knew saw me there? What if the guy turned out to be dangerous or something? It felt like if I backed down, I was giving in to my fear, and then I'd never be able to follow through on my larger plan.

The bowling alley at the casino was extremely crowded. It was jam-packed with bowling lanes, snack bars, gambling machines, and a video arcade. There was a thick smell of smoke and that indefinable, antiseptic aroma they put into the casino air system to hide the scent of fear and defeat. The high noise level seemed to make the whole environment seem anonymous, which gave me some comfort.

I saw Rico waiting at the appointed spot near the bowling lanes. He looked like a construction worker—about five-ten, 170 pounds, with short brown hair. He didn't look at all like what I pictured a male prostitute to be. He looked . . . I don't know . . . *normal*.

As I walked up to greet him, it occurred to me that this is just what Gacy would do, this is how he'd find someone to rape and kill. I was thinking about what Gacy might feel as he approached a prospective victim when Rico began the conversation.

"So what can I do for you?" he asked with a smile, as if we were both already well aware of what that might be.

"I was wondering," I started hesitantly, "I was wondering if I could pay you just to talk to me and give me some information about what you do."

The smile on Rico's face immediately froze, then turned downward into something not nearly as inviting. I quickly hurried on before he bolted altogether. "It's not what you think. I'm a student from UNLV and I want to write a paper about your lifestyle."

I could tell he was immediately suspicious. Maybe I was a cop? But I was too young to be a cop. More likely, he was guessing I really *did* want his services but was uncomfortable accepting my homosexuality.

Straight off, he wanted to eliminate his first suspicion. "Are you a cop," he asked, "or are you in any way related to someone in law enforcement?"

"No way," I reassured him. "I really just want to talk with you. Look," I said, showing him my student ID card.

He thought for a moment, then nodded. "For twenty dollars, I'll talk to you for a half hour. What do you want to know?"

"I really don't know where to start," I said as the two of us moved to a table. "I just need to know the basics about what you do. I need to know about the language you use and the terms for describing your various services."

He watched while I struggled with this. I was feeling very uncomfortable about the whole situation. Irrationally, I was sure I was going to run into someone I knew, and the next morning the TV would be broadcasting that I'd engaged the services of a male hooker.

Even more disturbing were the images that formed in my brain of what Rico did for a living. The very *idea* of two men having sex together stirred up some of my most conservative values, so much so that his taking money from almost anyone for his services seemed secondary. Vaguely, I wondered if I was being too judgmental.

Finally, I got right to the point and asked Rico what most of his customers asked for.

"Most guys just want to be blown," he said matter-of-factly. "Others want to be the top man."

"What's that?" I asked, having a feeling I knew.

"That's where they get to do me from behind. That costs the most. I get it all, though. Everything from guys paying to suck my dick to them paying me to fuck them up the ass."

I couldn't believe I was hearing this stuff! But I was very careful to maintain a blank expression. I could tell he was trying to shock me and I wouldn't give him the satisfaction of knowing how uncomfortable I was feeling.

"So," I continued, "how do you usually get propositioned?"

He then proceeded to educate me about the ins and outs, so to speak, of male prostitution. I learned the terms "hookers" and "Johns" use to describe their roles, how they recognize one another, what they do and how they do it. To tell you the truth, I was totally into this conversation. I couldn't believe how easy it was to pay someone for a half hour of his time and have him reveal the most bizarre, secret aspects of himself. I knew this was just what I needed to authenticate the character I was in the process of developing.

There was one aspect of the solicitation game that especially interested me because that would be the part of Gacy's world I'd most need to know about. I wasn't sure how to approach the subject diplomatically, so I just asked Rico straight out: "Did anyone ever try to hurt you?"

He pulled out a cigarette and looked thoughtful. "You'd be surprised how often that happens. Guys try a lot, but you have to be ready for it." Although he was acting as if being in constant jeopardy was no big deal, I could tell it really bothered him. After a pause, he continued. "One guy hit me over the head with a club as soon as I got into his car. He said he thought I looked like some guy who robbed him, but I just got the hell out of there. Another time, a guy put a knife to my throat while I was blowing him."

"Were you scared?" I asked him, frightened myself just hearing the story.

"Fuck yeah! I was thinking about biting his dick completely off. Fuck that cocksucker!" He was angry all over again, just thinking about the incident.

"So how did you get out of that situation?"

"I thought I'd just be able to bail out of there, but I was wrong. After I blew him, he fuckin' pissed on me."

Very naively, I asked him what he meant.

"He said, 'If you fucking move, I'll slice your throat.' Then he made me open my mouth and he pissed inside. He did manage to cut the side of my neck from the force of him holding the knife against it. Look at the scar."

Rico then showed me the scar as he continued. "I was so mad at that motherfucker. I wanted to kill him. If I ever see him again, I got a forty-five waiting to cap his ass."

"So how did you escape the guy?" I asked, completely captivated by his story. Listening to this guy was far better than reading about this world any day.

Rico seemed to have had enough of the conversation. We'd now run over the agreed-upon half hour anyway. He looked at me directly and asked, "Does this talk turn you on? I'd fuck you if you want to experiment. A lot of guys will pay me, and still won't admit they're fags."

"No. I'm not gay," I told him. "This really is just for school."

Well, at least the first part was truthful. I didn't feel too bad, though, because Rico had been fairly paid for his time.

For what I had in mind, it was important that I be able to speak convincingly in a way that Gacy would never question. I knew I had to be careful in everything that I wrote because I figured he had nothing to do all day except carefully scrutinize every word that arrived by letter.

So much for my strategy. I had more research to do, more interviews, more reading, more reflecting on how I would craft the first letter to attract Gacy's attention.

As I look back at all that unfolded during the next year, there's no way I could have possibly predicted what would result from this first step. It never occurred to me as I was creating a means to manipulate, control, and open up a collection of the world's most notorious serial killers that it would be I who was ultimately controlled and manipulated.

6

A Question of Motive

People always ask me why I do things that, to any normal person, are "over the top." Though self-analysis is only as good as the analyzer, let me try to take a stab at explaining my motivation.

Fear is a big theme in my life. Always has been. And every time I confront someone or something that makes me uneasy, my second impulse (after stifling the urge to run) is to study the source of my anxiety in an attempt to control it.

As regards this plan to gain the confidence of several serial killers, it felt like if I could fool someone like Gacy, if I could manage him and others like him, then I'd be protected against harm. This was magical thinking, I know—even irrational. But when this whole thing began, this was the only motive I could clearly articulate to myself even if it didn't satisfy others. "Tell me again, Jason," I often heard from friends, "why are you wasting your time preparing to write letters to killers, instead of coming with us to the party?"

What I realized is that the only answer people would accept was that I was working on a research project for school. In fact, this turned out to be true.

For my political science class, we had to do a research paper on some facet of the discipline. We had a brief section on capital punishment in the textbook, so I figured if I asked some actual killers how they felt about the subject, it might add some legitimacy to what was otherwise a pretty harebrained scheme. I also figured that, given the unique quotes that would be layered in, the paper couldn't help earning a high grade.

After class one afternoon, I decided to run my idea past the professor to see what he thought. I could feel the presence of two or three other students behind me, listening, as I described what I had in mind.

"Professor Gillman, I was thinking about doing my research paper on capital punishment and—"

"Well, that's great," he interrupted me. "But the paper is not due until four months from now." He was dismissing me and already moving on to the next student.

I hurriedly continued. "I know, but I usually like to get an early start." I had his attention again. "What I want to know is if it would be all right if I focused the paper on capital punishment from the prisoners' viewpoint?"

"What do you mean?" he asked.

"I was going to write some condemned killers and find out as much as I could about how they felt on the issue. I thought that would be a unique angle, and would make for an interesting paper. Don't you think?"

He didn't seem impressed. In fact, he looked annoyed, although I had no idea why. "I think there's enough research out there on capital punishment without you doing all this unnecessary poking."

Poking, I remember thinking. Is that all I'd be doing?

I could see the other students staring at me. They seemed surprised as much by my early start on the term paper as by my choice of subject. One of the guys turned to me and asked, "So who are you going to write to?"

I shrugged off the question. I knew where this conversation would lead. And I'd taken enough hits already from my family and friends.

"Jason, come on! What's the *real* reason you want to talk to these killers?" my buddies would tease. Or they'd call out to me across campus: "Hey, Jason, get any letters from Manson lately?"

Then they'd giggle and I'd laugh back, all the while stifling my irritation. But how could I blame them? I never took the time to really explain the *why* of it all. Maybe because I was afraid to confront it.

When I was totally honest with myself, I realized that part of the reason I was reaching out to these killers was that I *admired* them. Not for their crimes certainly—their behavior was beyond reprehensible—but for their nerve and follow-through. Not only did they dare to spit in the face of the rules that govern all people everywhere, but they did it *repeatedly,* as if taunting those who would try to control them.

At a time in my life when I was naturally experiencing some tension between what was expected of me—the "right path"—and a building urge to make my mark in a unique way, it was easier for these killers' actions to evoke in me a kind of awe.

Only later, after it was all over, would I realize the truth: that the perversion I read about—and ultimately witnessed—was weakness masquerading as strength.

I'd always known that there is a close link between criminals and those who catch them. I'd heard interviews in which police officers confided that they could have easily gone the other way if they'd gotten different breaks. And of course, there's the phenomenon in which serial killers often find ways to get close to the police and pretend to be officers themselves. I suspected that criminals and law enforcement officials have something in common—a taste for living on the edge. And if I was to ever become someone who could bring these killers to justice, I needed to better understand my own dark side.

Unfortunately, the journey I was beginning turned out to be very time-consuming. As important as it was for me to do well my first semester, I spent the next month reading everything I could get my hands on about my first subject, John Wayne Gacy. I read not only the few books written about him but also hundreds of articles. I watched video of interviews he'd given. I read the transcripts of his trial. Finally, I studied the profile of Gacy's victims, including their physical characteristics, their interests and personalities, their ages, and sexual preferences.

Putting everything I could find together, I concluded that Gacy was a man who thrived on power and control. He was a sexual sadist who reveled in the pain of others. He was absolutely brutal and merciless with his victims and yet could be incredibly charming when he chose. He was an expert manipulator, choosing victims who were emotionally weak, sexually confused, and vulnerable. Most of all, he seemed to underestimate his victims, and I felt certain I could use that to my advantage.

When I viewed videotapes of Gacy, I noticed that he seemed confident and cocky. He always had an answer for everything, including what the two dozen bodies were doing beneath his home.

"It beats me," he'd say, shrugging. "Someone else must have put them there. If I'm guilty of anything, it's operating a funeral home without a license." Then he'd flash a smug smile.

That overconfidence could be used against him, I figured. Gacy looked down on young boys, especially "gay boys." Given that's what I'd be posing as, I thought I could hold my own.

I recalled several other times in my life when adults had underestimated me. I remembered one day, soon after I'd received my driver's license, when I was driving down a road at moderate speed and a guy pulled right in front of me and made a U-turn. I put on the brakes but still couldn't avoid the inevitable collision.

The driver of the other vehicle immediately jumped out.

"What the hell do you think you're doing?" he yelled.

"Sorry, sir," I replied. "The road was slippery. I couldn't stop."

"The hell you couldn't. Shit. Look at my fuckin' truck!"

At that point, I didn't say a word. I just kept my head down, stared at my feet, and waited for the cops to arrive. I knew absolutely nothing would be solved by talking to this angry guy who was obviously going to paint a false picture of what happened.

"Fuckin' kids on the roads," he screamed into the night. "God damn it!" Then he looked at me. "You're insured, ain't ya? You're going to pay for this, ya know? You better have goddamn insurance!"

I remained quiet, just nodding my head when it seemed

appropriate. I wanted this guy to know as little as possible about me.

The police finally arrived at the scene. One officer approached us while the other surveyed the damage to both our vehicles.

"Okay, guys, what happened here?" the officer asked, shifting his eyes around to take in the scene.

"Look," the other driver said as he pointed at his truck, "this kid smacked right into me when I was trying to make a U-turn. He came from nowhere, going way over the speed limit. Didn't even see me. He must be drunk or something. He might even be retarded; he doesn't even talk."

As I listened to this story I couldn't help smiling to myself. Mr. U-Turn was digging himself in deeper and deeper.

The officer eyeballed me. "Well, son, is that what happened?"

"Not exactly, Officer," I replied calmly. Then in a confident, methodical way, I proceeded to explain my version of what occurred. "Actually, for me to have been speeding, the damage to both of our vehicles would have been a lot more severe. As you can see, the damage is minimal."

The driver looked stunned. I didn't seem at all like the passive, stupid kid he'd been screaming at a few minutes earlier.

"From the skid marks evident here," I continued, pointing to the road, "you can see that, in fact, I *did* see the vehicle way ahead of time and made an effort to stop." I continued on in defense-attorney style for another minute.

By the time I'd finished, the cop figured he had a handle on the situation. "Come here," he yelled to his partner, who was still examining the vehicles. "You gotta hear this one. You won't believe it."

The last I saw of Mr. U-Turn, they were giving him four separate citations and lecturing him about lying to the police.

That type of incident was not unusual in my life. Early on, I recognized the value of pretending to be dumber than I really was. I liked to watch people, to study their tendencies, to let them reveal the best they were capable of, and also the worst. Then I had a way to protect myself if they tried to hurt me.

For as long as I could remember, I'd had a hard time trusting people. I'm not sure why, but I believed that, given the chance, almost everyone would try to hurt me. It may have been those true-crime stories I was raised on. Or just an unlucky string of run-ins. Certainly, the messages I got from my parents were conflicting and confusing.

My mother, in particular, seemed completely unpredictable. One time she gave me a hundred dollars to go to the mall and buy new sneakers. I hadn't had a new pair of shoes in over two years, and she wanted to reward me because she felt I'd been behaving well—meaning that I'd done everything she asked of me and hadn't challenged her.

I was so excited when I walked in the door with my brand-new Nikes. "Mom, check these out!"

She looked at me but didn't say a word, so I said again, "Mom, come look at my shoes."

"Are you happy now? Are you happy, Jason, that you always get what you want?"

I couldn't believe what was happening. I knew I couldn't have done anything wrong because I hadn't even been home. All I'd done was go out to get the new shoes like she said I could.

"What are you talking about?" I asked.

"You're totally selfish! Your father's all upset that I let you spend so much money on shoes." Ah, so that explained it. "What the hell do you do around the house?" she continued. "Nothing! You get everything you want. You're a spoiled little brat. You just think you're the king, don't you?"

To this day, I'm still not able to predict when my mom's mood will change. But in her defense, I *can* be difficult at times—stubborn, surly, and yes, manipulative. It just amazed her that I was able to get away with the things I did, without paying what she believed was a fair price.

I'd somehow always known how to get people to open up, to tell me things they'd never admit to anyone else. I knew just what buttons to push, and once I had the information stored up, I felt armed in case they lashed out.

Reflecting on it, I think I employed this strategy with everyone else because I couldn't do it with my mother. She rarely told me anything about herself, but she demanded that I tell her *everything* about what was going on in my life. And each time we got into a fight, she used whatever I'd confided to her against me. Given the circumstances, it's not surprising I was unwilling to trust others, or that I constantly wore a mask to hide my true self.

7

Perfection and Fear

I was the firstborn son in my family, the first grandchild, the first nephew among my many uncles, and the first child among all of my parents' friends.

"He was spoiled rotten," my mother would tell anyone who asked about me. "He was doted on by everyone. Because he was constantly surrounded by other adults, he was always the center of attention. They played games with him and always let him win. To this day, Jason can't stand losing. He will do anything to make sure he is the one in control."

Needless to say, this was a sore point in our relationship. Winning was not just a game for me; it was as if my whole life was at stake every time I was asked to perform: whether playing a game, taking a test, or participating in a discussion. I had to be the best at everything I tried.

During my early school years, I was a model student—not only in my grades but in my citizenship. There was one elementary school teacher who deducted "points" for the least infraction, whether it was a late homework assignment or talking out of turn. Over the course of an entire year, I managed to avoid a single demerit, a feat the teacher found incredible if not troubling.

"I very much enjoy having Jason in my class," she explained during one parent conference.

"So what's the problem, then?" my mother replied.

"It's not really a problem so much as it's an area of concern."

"What's that supposed to mean?" my father pressed.

"Well, it just seems that Jason is very diligent about making sure he does everything in class exactly right. In fact, I've never seen anything quite like this."

She then described her point system and the many things a child could do that would result in a lost point. "Most kids, you see, lose a point here and there for their handwriting, or talking without raising their hands, or forgetting to turn in a homework assignment. That kind of thing. Your son, though, has never lost a point for anything!"

The looks of confusion on my parents' faces immediately transformed into gigantic smiles. Rather than be surprised by this report, they were relieved to hear I was continuing my perfect record.

"No, no," the teacher continued. "You misunderstand. I mean, you should be proud that Jason's work is excellent. My concern is that he is a little *too* diligent. It's just not altogether healthy for someone so young to be concerned with doing everything perfectly."

My parents finally got what the teacher was talking about. They'd also been bewildered by similar behavior at home. My father blurted out, almost without thinking, "You know, it would be good for him to lose a point here and there, just so he can get used to the idea. Maybe he'd loosen up a little."

The teacher agreed. From that remark, a plan was born in which it was decided that sometime during the upcoming week, she would manufacture some arbitrary reason for deducting a point.

But it wasn't until the next report that I became aware of my demerit. I couldn't believe it! I cried and sulked for days, devastated by my perceived failure. Even after my parents revealed that the teacher did this deliberately to teach me an important lesson, I still couldn't forgive myself for the lapse. I genuinely believed that if I'd done a better job, the teacher couldn't have found a single slip, no matter how hard she tried. Such was my misguided sense of proportion that for years afterward, it still bothered me that I'd lost that point. If I learned a lesson from the experience, it was to work even harder toward perfection.

But it wasn't enough to just work hard, I had to stand out! As the years flew by, the pattern became fixed: I craved attention—especially when it derived from overcoming some obstacle—but once I'd achieved my desired goal, the lack of challenge led me to a new project.

For example, I was always good at baseball. As an eleven-year-old third baseman, I was considered one of the most promising athletes in the city, invited to play in leagues with much older boys. One year later, to the surprise of my family and friends, I abruptly quit. I told people that I just didn't feel like it was enough of a challenge any longer.

Looking back, the real reason I quit was that I was afraid of being second best. There were other boys who were bigger, stronger, and faster than I was. Before long, they'd be able to perform better than I could, no matter how hard I worked. I just couldn't stand the thought of that. I'd rather not play at all than face the prospect that I wasn't the absolute best.

The following year I took up the trumpet, eventually ascending to second chair in the school band. The music teacher felt that I had great potential as a musician, but I soon lost interest in the instrument. I just couldn't see myself in a high school marching band. I intended to be the star football player.

Along with these athletic pursuits, I also had a number of hobbies, especially collecting things. When most boys my age were collecting baseball cards, I became a dealer. I got a job in a card store just so I could have a first look at anything new that came in. On occasion, I would also accost younger kids on the street to try to buy their collections.

Before that, it was a huge coin collection. I taped coins to every spare sheet of paper in the house. I attended coin shows, wrote to family members all over the country recruiting their assistance to search for particular pennies I especially coveted. I visited the mint in Philadelphia to get more rare and unique coins. And just like everything else I did, once I felt I'd met the challenge, I moved on to something else.

When I was fifteen, I took up weight lifting with a vengeance. I became completely obsessed with bulking up my body. I worked out two, even three times a day, to the point where I was huge—over 200 pounds at five feet, eight inches tall. I reached a point where I was eating dozens of vitamin supplements, taking weight-gainer fuel, as well as eating half a loaf of bread for breakfast each day.

Eventually, this, too, became boring, so I moved on to kickboxing. Again, I became totally focused on being the absolute best. I went to school, then to the gym, then to kickboxing, and finally fell into bed exhausted each night. This used to drive my parents nuts.

"Jason," my mother would vent, "is there some reason why we have to live with that pole thing in the yard?"

That "pole thing" was a gigantic stake I'd sunk into the ground to use for toughening up my feet and legs for tournaments. I'd kick it for hours at a time.

"Come on, Mom, you know I need it to get myself ready."

"I just don't know what to do with you. You use those bottles to rub your shins till they're raw. You—"

"I told you a hundred times. I have to deaden the nerve endings on my legs—"

"Don't use that tone of voice with us!" my father would object.

"Look, Jason," my mother would warn, "we've had just about enough of this stuff!" and the lecture would continue.

As a little boy, I continuously lived with fears of being abandoned, as well as being kidnapped. I cried a lot. From kindergarten onward, I presented an image of being well behaved but unusually vulnerable.

My parents tried to shelter me as much as possible. Whereas my friends were allowed to see scary movies, I was never permitted to do so. In fact, even certain news shows and documentaries were ruled out.

At age seven, I remember lying in bed one night, trying to get to sleep, and hearing the sound of the television in the other room. By the sounds of the screaming and music, I could tell that my parents were watching something frightening.

I snuck out of bed and peered down the hallway to see

what was being broadcast. It turned out to be a film about the Holocaust. I sat in the darkened hallway, huddled on the floor, and witnessed Nazi soldiers beating and killing people. I saw dead bodies being moved around and piled up in stacks. I couldn't figure out why anyone would treat others that way. I wondered what bad things the skinny people had done to deserve such brutal treatment.

While I sat frozen in the hallway, shuddering and frightened, my parents turned and discovered what I'd been up to. The look on my face was enough to confirm their worst fears about why they should continue to shield me from such horror.

"Come here, honey," my mother called out. I thought I was in big trouble for sneaking out of bed.

My dad, as well, seemed unusually solicitous at a time when I would normally be yelled at. My tears seemed to be working, in part because my terror was genuine.

"Hitler is dead," my father explained. "The Nazis lost the war. They can't hurt you now."

"But we're Jewish, too, just like the people in that movie."

"Yes, that's true," my father admitted, "but people are not like that anymore. That's why Grandpa went in the army, to stop that type of thing."

Once calmed down, I was filled with questions. "But why did the Nazis want to kill Jewish people? Did they do something bad?"

"No, honey, the Nazis were bad people and they liked to hurt others." Even as he was uttering the words, my father knew that such a simple explanation would never satisfy me.

"But why did they do that? Why did they kill people? Will people try to kill us, too? Mom, I don't want to die."

I had so many questions, and I hoped some answers might appease my fear. I was especially curious about what the soldiers thought about when they killed the Jews. I wondered how they slept at night and whether they had nightmares about the things they'd done.

My parents tried to answer my questions as patiently as they could, but I exasperated them. They just wanted a normal kid who wasn't so sensitive, so inquisitive. Never in their wildest dreams could they imagine how far my curiosity would take me.

8

Monsters

I've always felt drawn to that which I fear the most, especially when it's forbidden. When I was ten years old, I earned first place in a science-fair competition, an honor that allowed me to enter an advanced placement course offered by the school system. Told to choose a special project for the year, I begged my teacher to let me dissect a frog. Then I badgered my parents to give me permission. Against their better judgment, they acquiesced. I couldn't wait for the momentous day.

My mother accompanied me to the proceeding, since she was also interested in what a dissection would be like. As soon as we walked into the lab, I could smell the sickening stench of formaldehyde.

At one end of the room were science supplies—skeletons, tubes, beakers, and the like—and at the other were four long brown wooden tables. One table, in the opposite corner of the room, looked like it had been set aside for us. There were chairs all around it, and a large pan in the middle surrounded by dissecting tools.

"Jason, this is going to be so much fun for you," my

mother whispered as she put her arm around me. "How many other kids at your age get to dissect a frog?"

"Yeah," I agreed, not at all sure what I was in for. I wasn't exactly feeling well. Probably just some jitters from anticipating the happy event.

As we walked toward the table, the teacher of advanced studies, Miss Pernatozzi, soon followed behind. She was a little woman, probably only about five feet tall. She had a high-pitched voice, which always made it seem as if she was overly excited.

"Okay, guys," she ordered us, "have a seat. I'll be right back. I need to get something real quick. Try to familiarize yourself with the frog." She pointed to the green lump in the middle of the pan. "I left a sheet there for you to see where you'll find all the major organs and structures."

"This is neat," my mother said excitedly, and nudged me.

I now got my first look at the frog. It was lying on its back, belly up, on this waxy substance. The smell was even stronger and more putrid than when we first entered the room. The legs of the poor little creature were pinned into the wax with long needles. There was no way this frog was going to move, even if it was alive. Somehow this reassured me.

Miss Pernatozzi walked back in and told us about the procedures we were going to be following.

"First, we'll make an incision here," she said, pointing to a spot on the frog. I was trying to hold my breath so I didn't have to inhale that terrible smell.

"Then," my teacher continued, "we'll be pulling this out from there . . ."

I could feel my stomach tighten as she described what

we were to do. I felt like I had something in my eyes. Maybe dirt or something. I don't know, but things were a little blurry.

"Okay, Jason," she said, "are you ready to make the first cut?" I looked at my mother pleadingly. She could tell I was a little apprehensive.

Since I didn't move, my mother suggested that perhaps the teacher could show us how to get started.

"All right," Miss Pernatozzi agreed.

She picked up the scalpel and began making an incision along the length of the frog's stomach. My mother was looking intently at what she was doing. I felt like a warm blanket had been thrown over me. I was beginning to feel very hot. And I was doing everything I could to look anywhere but at this frog that was in the process of being disemboweled.

"Jason," my mother said, "watch what she's doing right now. You'll be doing this in a minute, so pay attention."

I looked back down again and saw Miss Pernatozzi peeling the flesh of the frog's stomach back and pinning it against the wax. I couldn't take it anymore.

"Jason?" my mother asked. "Jason . . . are you okay?"

I began to see a white fuzz all around, like the screen of a television that has no signal coming through. Everything around me seemed to be shaking violently.

The next thing I knew, I was on the floor. I could hear echoes of my mother's voice, calling my name. "Jaaason . . . Jaason." I opened my eyes and found myself on the floor in my mother's lap. I'd fainted and fallen off the chair.

I was covered in sweat, and very scared and confused. I could hear Miss Pernatozzi in the background say, "I guess I'll start putting these things away."

I felt *so* embarrassed. So ashamed. They went through all this effort for me and I didn't even have the stomach to go through with it. Since that time, I've always been repulsed by the least sight of blood. So much for a career in medicine.

Although I won the Presidential Academic Fitness Award at age eleven, I was still viewed by my parents as being weak and vulnerable. Hence, I wasn't permitted to view anything on television or in the movies that might upset my weak stomach. This especially rankled when a movie was released called *Friday the 13th.* I'd been told that it was about a guy who stalks others in the most horrifying way; ironically, he was named Jason! I reasoned that if I could face what I feared the most, a bogeyman-like monster trying to snatch and kill me, then perhaps I wouldn't be so afraid all the time.

I begged my parents to let me see the movie but my mother adamantly refused. I found this hypocritical because she was constantly reading her true-crime books and giving me capsule descriptions.

My fears weren't just based on fantasy. When I was little, my younger brother and I were waiting in one of the local casinos while our parents were doing a little recreational gambling. Jarrod and I were playing in the video arcade, where I was teaching him how to manipulate the controls.

While we were occupied with one of the games, a man approached us and sort of struck up a conversation.

"You're pretty good at that game," he said. "You must practice a lot."

"Thanks, I do," I answered shyly. I knew I wasn't supposed to talk to strangers but in this case I couldn't see any way to avoid it. Besides, he seemed nice enough.

"Jason," my brother said, tugging at me, "what do I do now?"

Normally, I'd be bugged by Jarrod's interrupting, but I was glad for the distraction. "Sorry, mister, but I gotta help my brother."

"That's okay, little guy. I just like watching you play."

I looked around the room helplessly. My parents were a million miles away. My brother had no idea what was going on. And this guy was getting more and more familiar with me. Now he was bumping into me and rubbing my shoulders.

"Uh, mister, we gotta go now. Our parents are waiting just over there." I pointed in the general direction of the casino, but he could tell I was lying.

"I'll tell you what, son, why don't you just come with me for a little while. I'll take you back to my house and we can play some games there together."

I froze. I knew my brother and I were in deep trouble. But every time I tried to move away from the man, he kept following us closely, touching me whenever he could.

What was even more annoying was that Jarrod was completely oblivious to the danger. "Come on, Jason, look at this! Look what I did!" He was so mesmerized by the flashing lights of the games that he wouldn't look at me long enough for me to signal him that we had to get out of there.

I thought I could get away from the guy if I was by myself, but there was no way I could do much with my little brother there. I saw the man looking around, checking to see who was watching us, when I punched my brother in the arm hard enough to make him cry.

Perfect. Jarrod was making some serious noise.

"That's not going to work," the man said to me with a smile. "You're still coming home with me."

"Okay, mister, I'll come with you, but I can't leave my brother like this. Let me just show him where my parents are so he doesn't get scared. Then I'll come with you."

I don't know if he bought my excuse or not. Maybe he just got nervous because he realized things were getting more complicated than he'd anticipated. But while he was thinking things over, I grabbed my brother's hand and started moving us toward the door. I whispered in his ear that a monster was after us so we'd better run for our lives. Jarrod thought I was kidding but we still shot out of there as fast as we could.

I didn't want my parents getting all excited, so I didn't tell them much about what happened—just that some guy scared us. I was curious, though, about why someone would want to snatch kids and hurt them. What was it about a person's background that fed such urges? I somehow connected that child molester in the casino with slashers in horror movies and, later, real-life serial killers.

I finally saw *Friday the 13th*—with two friends, and *without* my parents' permission. Just a few minutes into the film—when the eerie music first starts to rise, signaling impending doom—I closed my eyes, and I kept them tight until the closing credits. I didn't actually *see* the movie this first time, but hearing it was bad enough. Afterward, I had vivid nightmares in which a monster would stalk and try to kill me.

Even so, I went back to see the movie a second time, this time forcing myself to watch the whole gruesome spectacle. I figured the reality had to be more tolerable than the nightmares.

On some level I don't really understand, a part of me also enjoyed the feelings of panic and fear that we all recognize as the stimulation that draws us to such films in the first place. Once the lights come back on, we breathe a sigh of relief when we realize that our own sorry lives are not nearly as bad as we once imagined. What's a crummy job, or a fight with a friend, or a bad head cold, compared to being tortured by one of these monsters?

During the next year, I must have seen a hundred so-called slasher movies. Having been denied for so long, and having finally broken down my parents' resistance, I was going to jump into this hobby just like everything else I tried. Somewhere along the line, I even began enjoying the genre with its campy scripts and predictable story lines. I began to see real artistry in the director's ability to build tension and play with the audience's hunger for stimulation.

Being somewhat obsessive by nature, I proclaimed my new passion by covering the walls of my room with horror posters. I also subscribed to horror magazines and read horror comic books. I even suspended a fake dead body from the bedroom ceiling and perched toy skulls on every shelf and space I could find.

Some of my friends called me weird. And they were right. But I didn't care. I'd managed to transform my fear into fascination.

9

In Training

During my thirteenth year, I had my bar mitzvah and, in the Jewish tradition, "became a man," prompting my father to take me aside for a private talk. I wondered what was going on because he seemed especially nervous.

"Jason, now that you're no longer a boy, I have something for you."

Feeling him put something into my hand, I looked down and saw it was three Trojan condoms. "Thanks, Dad."

"This doesn't mean you need to rush out and use them," he pointed out, "but if you do have sex, make sure you use protection."

"I will," I assured him.

Soon after, I slipped one of the condoms into my wallet, hoping that by some miracle I'd get the opportunity to use it. I couldn't believe that a girl in my class actually accommodated me. Although it was really fun, and I was extremely careful to use the condom properly, I was terrified that I might have somehow gotten her pregnant. Again, my fears destroyed what was otherwise a great experience.

For a few weeks, I believed that all my hopes and

dreams for the future were over, that my life was ruined, all because I'd gotten a girl pregnant. Once I learned my fears were groundless, I resolved I wouldn't have sex again, a promise I kept until several years later when I became involved with a much older woman, the mother of a friend.

I think I was attracted to this older woman because of the challenge of getting her into bed. It was my competitive instinct flaring up again. Looking back on it now, even *I'm* amazed—and yes, a little embarrassed—by my audacity.

"Look," I remember saying to her, shortly after I signaled my interest, "I think that we want the same things out of life. Honesty and communication are the most important things in a relationship, don't you agree?"

"I suppose so," she said. "How *old* did you say you are again—*sixteen*?"

"But think about it," I continued, ignoring her. "What person is really going to say that he or she doesn't want those things? I really *mean* it. I want to be able to see you after you get off work, and by just the expression on your face, know exactly what you're thinking and feeling. I want you to be able to open up about anything, and never have to fear I'll judge you in any way."

From her expression, I could tell I had her attention, so I kept going. "I want a relationship where we can just be ourselves—say exactly what's on our minds. I want to know your every thought. I want to get as close to you as you'll let me."

I could see her actually move physically closer to me. She was staring intently into my eyes.

"You really know what you want, don't you?" she said, smiling. "I've never heard anyone speak the way you do."

Actually, she probably had. On a soap opera or something. That's probably what inspired me.

The funny thing, though, is that I meant every word. And the point of the story is that this sort of training—this attempt to become the type of person someone else finds appealing—would stand me in good stead when it came to my later project of befriending serial killers.

Even at school, I found loads of opportunities to do role-playing.

As far back as junior high school, I noticed that cliques formed along definite lines: preppies, geeks, stoners, jocks, and gangsters. I was fascinated with these various groups and wondered if it was possible to cross-fraternize, as it were. Being an honors student and athlete who never, ever got into trouble, I was especially interested in the bad kids, the weirdos, the ones everyone else shied away from.

I could never be bad, though I always found appealing the *reputation* of being bad, so it seemed that the next best thing was to hang out with some of these kids who got into fights, carried weapons, and had earrings hanging from every orifice. Understand, this was not easy for a clean-cut type like me to pull off. I had to find ways to get these kids to accept me without joining in their bad behavior.

One method I found effective was to learn the distinct languages of the groups I traversed. I would sit in the school cafeteria and survey the scene, noting where various groups were hanging out. Then I'd make my rounds.

"What up?" I'd say to some of my stoner friends huddled in a corner of the cafeteria.

"Hey," a few of them might answer back. "What's going down, man?"

"You guys look a little blazed right now. You're pretty fucked up, huh?"

They'd giggle. "Hey, man, you gotta do what ya gotta do."

"Yeah," I'd agree. "I bought a eighth last night for twenty. Good shit. Some really good fuckin' shit."

"Really? What's it laced with? Coke or something?"

That sort of insider question might trip me up, so I'd just nod, hoping an affirmation wouldn't set off any alarms.

"Well, man," I'd say, "I gotta bail now. Let's hook up later."

"Cool."

Next, I'd saunter over to another part of the cafeteria where the jocks were eating lunch and talking about their latest athletic exploits.

"You still training, Jason?" one of them might ask as I approached.

"Damn straight," I'd say. "Feel these arms."

At that point one of them could be counted on to grab my biceps and squeeze as hard as he could, trying to bring some pain.

After some more posturing and high-testosterone ribbing, I might see a teacher coming down the hall and choose to transform myself into another person altogether. Sometimes I'd do this all day, never growing tired of it, moving from one group to another.

The fact is, I enjoyed learning what made various people tick. As I've said previously, it armed me against potential threats, *and* it satisfied my curiosity.

During my last year of high school, I decided to learn about some of the most exotic people of all—transsexuals and transvestites. I thought they'd make an interesting topic for a paper I'd been assigned. I began to write individuals who described themselves as such, pretending to be one of them. In turn, they told me their stories, sent me pictures of themselves, and provided a wealth of information that proved invaluable when I began drafting letters to serial killers.

As part of my continued "training," I also began answering ads placed by heterosexual women. I'd carefully study what each was looking for and then describe myself in such a way as to get a response. Getting replies turned out to be easy, though, so I began looking for bigger challenges.

I suppose that's how I came round to my serial killer idea.

What bigger challenge was there than to try to outfox— and in the process learn about—someone who'd led police on a merry chase for years? As someone who considered himself an above-average but still amateur role-player, I could think of no greater turn-on than to go mano a mano with one of the country's most lethal—and clever—Jekyll and Hydes.

10

The Questionnaire

Just prior to Thanksgiving vacation I was finally ready to send off a letter to my first subject, John Wayne Gacy. Every word was carefully constructed to project the image of someone who was young, lonely, needy, and yet also very desirable. If I was correct, the total "package" would represent the same kind of irresistible temptation that had attracted Gacy on over two dozen separate occasions thirteen years before.

On November 24, 1993, I posted the following letter:

Dear Mr. Gacy,

    My name is Jason Moss, and I'm a full time college student at the University of Nevada, Las Vegas. I'm 18 years old, and I'm writing because I thought you might get bored or lonely where you are, and that you might want someone to correspond with. I'm sure there are many others who write you, but I hope you take the time to write me back. You'll see that I'm

a pretty nice guy, and I know what it's like
to be bored and alone. The constant screaming
of my father keeps me secluded in my room when
I'm not in school or at the gym. I hate it here
at home, and I guess I understand what it's
like to need a friend.

At this point I don't really know what else
to say until you write me back. If you should
need anything like paper or supplies, just let
me know. I would be happy to help. I look forward to hearing from you soon.

Your friend,
Jason Moss

I felt a tremendous relief after I sent the letter off; it was
out of my hands. There was nothing more I could do. I'd researched things as best I could. Now it was time for me to
get on with the rest of my life, which I'd been neglecting for
some time. I jumped back into schoolwork with my usual
zeal and also devoted extra time to my girlfriend, Jenn,
whom I'd been avoiding during the weeks leading up to
sending the letter.

Just seven days later, though, to my utter shock, a letter
arrived from the Menard Correctional Center in Illinois. I
hadn't expected to receive a reply so fast. The first thing I
did was run down the stairs to tell my mother the news.

"Can you believe it? Look who wrote me! John Wayne
Gacy wrote me back. I can't believe it!"

My mother looked up from the magazine she'd been
glancing through. "Great," she said without enthusiasm,
and resumed reading.

I stood there staring at her, the letter gripped tightly in my hand. She looked up again at me, as if she wondered what I was doing there. "So now you've got a new serial killer friend. You really worry me sometimes."

"Mom, don't you see how great this is!" I just couldn't restrain my excitement. "How many people can say they've received a letter from John Wayne Gacy?"

"Who'd want to brag about such a thing?" she countered, and again went back to the magazine.

Both my parents had been hoping that my latest obsession would go the way of dozens of others, and eventually fade out. But alas, now I would only be encouraged to continue this foolishness to wherever it might lead next.

Gacy's letter was only a paragraph long, typed double-spaced. The grammar and punctuation revealed his lack of education. He was brief and to the point in thanking me for writing. He included a few enclosures, a self-authored article that described his version of the events that led up to his arrest and conviction, and a questionnaire he wanted me to complete before the correspondence could go any further.

This survey, I later learned, was part of Gacy's standard operating procedure. It was the means by which he filtered out, from among the thousands of people who contacted him, a few fans to correspond with. The form contained dozens of items related to interests and preferences, such as "My childhood hero," "Why you wrote J. W. Gacy," "Ideal evening," and "Nobody knows about: _____." Yet hidden among these seemingly innocuous queries were also things like: "Thoughts on sex," "Thoughts on crime," and "What you're thinking now." These were the items I figured would be most significant to Gacy.

My initial elation now gave way to a certain anxiety.

Clearly, Gacy wasn't going to take at face value just anything that was sent to him. He may have been guilty of overconfidence but he wasn't stupid; he obviously planned to dig deep into the mind of whomever he befriended.

This project was going to be a lot more difficult than I'd ever imagined. While I welcomed the challenge of trying to plumb Gacy's mind, all the while blocking access to my true self, I also felt a lot of external pressure.

Although I was busy planning the next step in our correspondence, my parents were adamant about calling a halt to the whole thing.

"What are we supposed to tell our friends you're doing lately?" my mother complained. " 'Oh, nothing much. He's got a new friend, though. John Gacy. Perhaps you've heard of him? Tortured and killed thirty-three boys about Jason's age. But I understand he's very nice when he's in a good mood.' "

My father added his own concerns. "Don't you worry people might think you're a little strange, writing to killers?" Eventually realizing that his argument was falling on deaf ears, he pleaded, "Jason, why don't you start going back to the gym again?"

"Dad, I'm going to learn a lot of cool stuff if this works out. So what if other people wouldn't try this? You know I'm not like everyone else. Why are you trying to make me *act* like everyone else?"

One cool, fall night I followed my father outside so he could smoke a cigarette. We stood in the backyard, moving around to stay warm. "Jason," he said, "you're going to do whatever you want. I know that. But Mom doesn't like this idea, and it's going to cause trouble around the house. I can already feel it."

I felt sorry for him. He was always catching flak for the things I dreamed up.

"Dad, you know Mom is against almost everything I try. Why should this be any different? I promise I won't let it get out of hand."

But "out of hand" is what it eventually got.

The response from Gacy suggested that if I did my homework carefully, I could get inside the mind of *any-body*. Already, I started thinking about other serial killers I might contact, but I was getting ahead of myself: first I had to capture Gacy's interest.

I knew that my next hurdle was to get through his prim-itive "psychological test" in such a way that I'd not only "pass" but that he'd fight to be my mentor and teacher. I needed to fill out the items in such a way that I'd sound genuine and sincere, yet very confused and vulnerable.

I reviewed what I knew about Gacy, and what I sus-pected was the case. Although he claimed to be bisexual, I knew that he'd stopped having sex with women just about the time he began his two-year killing spree. As for what I suspected: obviously, he'd be against the death penalty, he'd have some fairly liberal attitudes about sex, and he'd be especially attracted to someone who was easily con-trolled.

I crafted my responses with the same meticulous care that I devoted to a pivotal term paper. One question asked me about my impression of the "perfect man or woman." I crossed out "woman" and wrote in "partner" instead, so it would seem that I might be inclined toward bisexuality or homosexuality. I added that my partner would have to be kind, sensitive, sincere, funny, and good-looking. I tried to make my responses as ambiguous as I could so I'd have some flexibility later to alter my beliefs, depending on what evolved. I was really just operating in the dark, even though I'd gathered some good intelligence.

There was one question that began: "Nobody knows I'm _____." I decided I should throw in something provocative to get his wheels spinning. I answered: ". . . thinking about being a nude dancer to earn extra money." In my mind, this accomplished the following: First, it let him know that I had an attractive body and wasn't inhibited about flaunting it. Second, it suggested I wasn't above *selling* my body—which, undoubtedly, would play into his incredible rage toward boy hustlers. I remembered, for example, that a hustler by the name of Donald Voorhees was responsible for Gacy's early conviction for sodomy. Thereafter, from what I could determine, most of Gacy's victims shared physical characteristics with Voorhees.

I tried to answer every item on the questionnaire in a way that I believed would entice Gacy. I was like a fly fisherman who'd felt the tiniest tug on the line, and was trying to shake the fly in a way that would get the fish to take the hook.

11

Setting Bait

It had been several days since I'd mailed in the questionnaire and I wondered how long it would take for Gacy to reply. I've never been patient during the best of times and this was positively agonizing.

I'm a compulsive worrier and I agonized over the responses I eventually settled on. Maybe I shouldn't have said something about my parents so quickly. I could think of a dozen other responses I wished I'd constructed differently. *What if he doesn't write back?*

While the wait continued, I thought about the other killers I wanted to contact. As a preliminary step toward writing them, I tried to obtain addresses for some of the more famous Death Row inmates—a task that turned out to be far easier than I anticipated. Charles Manson, in particular, was fairly simple to track down, so I started reading a bit about him as a way to keep myself occupied.

Since I'd been unable to persuade my parents that becoming a serial killer's pen pal was "cool," I made it a point to leave school promptly every afternoon so I could intercept the mail. I figured I'd have a clear shot at it, given that my parents were always at work, and my brother was at school. After a few days I developed the habit of sitting in a rocking chair in my parents' room, which faced the street, waiting for the mail truck to come.

Our mail lady, Cynthia, was utterly dependable, never varying more than a few minutes from her usual arrival time. This was especially important because I was cutting things very close. There were times my mother would come home from work only a few minutes after I'd sorted through the mail.

"Well, Jason," Cynthia said one day after finding me standing by the mailbox, "this might just be your lucky day." We had become fast friends and I'd confided to her the sort of thing I was looking for. She tilted her head in the direction of the top letter on the stack of our mail. Clearly typed at the top of the envelope was the return address: Menard Correctional Center.

All riiiiight!

I read through the letter, which was quite long, quickly the first time, just to get the main ideas Gacy was expressing. He seemed to be trying to make it clear that he was a very open and safe person. He wanted me to know that I could confide in him about anything, and he was obviously hoping I'd do so.

It was strange to read Gacy's words—to think that this man, who'd taken the lives of so many young men just like me, was now turning his attention my way. I could feel a chill that reminded me of the first time I watched *Friday the 13th* all the way through. All the time you're watching the movie, hearing that scary music, seeing the unsuspecting kid about to get decapitated, you want to scream out: "You idiot! Get the hell out of there! Can't you sense that monster about to devour you?" I felt like I might be in a movie as well, and I wondered, if an audience *were* watching, whether they'd scream out for me to throw the damn letter down and run for my life.

One part of Gacy's letter, in particular, caught my attention because of the subtle ways he was trying to get me to open up to him, especially with regard to my sexual attitudes and behavior:

> . . . One of the things you should know about me, is that I am open minded, outspoken, not very tactful, nonjudgmental, liberal, BI [bisexual], and I say what I mean. The only thing I ask is don't assume anything of me. If your not sure then ask. Nothing offends me and nothing is personal. No subject is off limits as long as your willing to be just as open and honest with me. I dislike phoney people. 80% of what is known about me in the media is fantasy. So don't assume, just ask. If you want my opinion on something or point of view thats what you will get as I am not into stroking you as you have your own hand for that when you get the daily urge. Ha ha.

The letter continued on for a half dozen pages, during which he talked about my answers to his questionnaire and prodded me for more details. He was especially interested in anything I had to say about my sexual experience and fantasies. He kept reassuring me that he was a safe confidant and that I should tell him anything and everything I'd ever thought or felt.

Relax about who will see what you write as
I don't share my letters with anyone and even
if you stand on your head to jack off, I would
say go for it as I am not into judging someone else. Same with being a male stripper. In
fact maybe you could explain that liberal side
of you that you seem protective of. Hey, life
is an adventure and as long as its consenting
and you feel good about it then go for it.

I felt the beginnings of confusion even as early as this
second letter. If I didn't know who this guy was, or what he
did, I would have found him, despite the sexual innuendo,
interesting—even engaging. Since I was feeling somewhat
alienated and lonely, I almost welcomed his offer of friendship. I admit this only with the greatest reluctance; the more
rational part of me was well aware of what he was trying to
do and realized he wasn't the slightest bit interested in my
welfare. Gacy's game was to find a little diversion in his
otherwise restricted, boring life stuck in a cell twenty-three
hours a day.

Studying the letter more thoroughly, I noticed the many
references to masturbation. This would become a common
theme in Gacy's letters as he jumped from one subject to
the next, and then abruptly started talking about sex in the
most provocative and disgusting way he could. I found this
pornographic streak especially difficult to take. Although I
was certainly no prude, I did have a fairly idealized view of
sex, and it certainly didn't include sadomasochistic or incestuous practices. I felt secure in my own heterosexual inclinations, but the constant references to homosexuality

were unsettling because in my role-playing guise I'd be forced to grapple with them.

I assumed from his letter that my answers to his questionnaire intrigued him and that he wished to know more. He seemed to be defending himself, letting me know that what I probably knew about him was just media sensationalism. The message was clear: to learn the truth—Gacy's truth—I'd need to ask him directly.

At this point I knew I had Gacy's attention, but the question was, for how long? I had no idea how many others were competing for his time and attention. To ensure that I remained his focus, I decided, in my next letter, to continue modeling myself on his "ideal victim" by painting myself as both sexually active and submissive.

December 12, 1993
Dear John,

I will be honest with you. I AM a very liberal person. I wrote modestly because I was afraid that you would show my letters to others. Since you said you would not do that, I will be more relaxed with you in writing. When I was discussing sex, I stated that I was interested in trying a lot of different things. Although I haven't tried much myself, I have an open mind to try many different things. Right now there is an older woman who keeps forcing herself on me. She is one of my mother's friends, and last week she told me to go down on her. I felt uncomfortable, and just wanted to do as she said. I was afraid to cause any trouble.

Well, I will not bore you with that problem. John, I know we just started corresponding, but I was wondering how you felt about writing me. I think you are a great guy, and I am really taking a personal interest in the letters you write me. I hope it is the same on your part. Is it?

Like I mentioned to you before, I really want us to become friends, and for you to say what is on your mind. I don't always want to ask you specific questions, I would rather you just volunteer information as the thoughts go through your head, good or bad. . . . The only other things I would like to know about you are the ideas, thoughts, and emotions that enter your mind. (Boring or exciting, it does not matter to me, I am truly fascinated and interested in the things you think about.) It does not matter if your letters become 20 pages long, I am interested, and it is very important to me. (As long as you feel comfortable with it of course.)

Your friend,
Jason Moss

In retrospect, I was naive to think that Gacy would confide in me by letter secrets he'd never told anyone before, or that he might even confess his crimes. But it did seem to me that if I could just get him comfortable with airing his thoughts, he'd reveal things indirectly.

Gacy's immediate reply included the following:

> I will say one thing. Your letters sound like that you would be much older than your 18 years, soon to be 19. You come across very responsible in how you speak. I have a saying—don't say it unless you intend on doing it and you come across as if you mean to do what you say, and that to me is being honest with yourself.

Even though I knew Gacy was playing with me, I was nevertheless flattered. Just as I'd selected *him* out of hundreds of Death Row predators to write to, he'd selected *me* to focus on out of hundreds of academics, voyeurs, and would-be disciples vying for his attention.

I'd earned the devil's nod.

12

Secrets

At the time, my bedroom looked like most any other male teenager's inner sanctum, decorated in a way that reminded an unwary interloper—my mother, for example—that the hormones were abundantly flowing. I had a poster on one of my walls of two beautiful women bent over on the beach. Its caption read: "California Beach Bums." On the opposing wall was an assortment of other cheesecake shots that I'd cut out of *Playboy*.

There was actually a *floor* in my room, but the joke in our house was that nobody had seen it in years. Strewn around the room, covering every available inch, were dirty clothes, as well as clean clothes that I'd taken out and planned to wear sometime in the near future. Books were stacked everywhere, reflecting my diverse interests: school books, library books, and of course my growing collection of works about serial killers.

I was seated at my desk around midnight, furiously typing away at the computer, when a knock at the door cut through my concentration.

"Come in," I grunted.

"Jason," my father whispered, poking his head through the door, "it's awfully late. Are you going to be able to get up for school tomorrow?"

"Yeah. I'm just working on another letter." By this point my parents were resigned to my "project." Even so, I downplayed the number of letters that were flying back and forth and continued intercepting the mail every afternoon.

"Well," he replied, "I'm getting ready for bed. Make sure you turn off all the lights downstairs and don't forget to let the dog out. He's been having accidents all over the house lately. Mom's probably going to take him to the vet tomorrow."

"Okay, Dad," I mumbled, only half listening as I continued typing.

My father stood in the doorway watching me for a minute. Almost against his will, he asked, "So how's the letter writing going? Is he liking what you have to say?"

"I hope so," I responded noncommittally. I didn't know how much my father really wanted to know. I could tell he was really curious about what I was up to, but if I told him too much, it might lead to trouble with my mom. I decided to give him a general idea without too many specifics.

"I just try to imagine what he'd want to hear. That's what I tell him."

My father nodded. "Well, if anyone can do that, it's you."

I wasn't quite sure if that was a compliment or not. I preferred to think that in his own way my father was telling me he was proud of what I was doing even if he didn't understand it all.

"Thanks, Dad," I said. "Good night. I'll see you in the morning."

Practically speaking, the real curse of responding to Gacy's letters had become the amount of research and reflection it required. Sometimes I'd stay up until four in the morning, writing and rewriting each sentence. I had to cross-reference everything I told him because I knew he'd notice the slightest inconsistency in my story. After all, he had nothing to do all day except to try to suppress thoughts of his upcoming execution; I knew my letters would be a welcome distraction and that he'd study them intently.

Sometimes Gacy would try to turn the tables and trick *me*—or at least it felt that way. He'd say, remember three weeks ago when you said you were wearing a red shirt? How come you didn't mention that shirt again? I knew then that Gacy had his own index system, that he remembered everything I ever told him.

I tried to be objective as I went through every line I created. How would he interpret this? What would it trigger? Is this what my fictitious character would think or feel or say? I made sure that every letter that went out was a masterpiece of subtlety, yet be a lever that opened Gacy up just a little bit more. It was ridiculously time-consuming.

While previously I'd always been a perfect student, for the first time I was about to get Bs in my first-semester classes. I became so preoccupied, so obsessed with my serial killer project, that I let everything else slip in my life—not only school but romantic relationships, friendships, and athletic pursuits. It occurred to me that *I* might be the one who was hooked, not Gacy.

One night I was sitting on the couch in the living room staring at the blank television screen, a biology book open on my lap, when I heard footsteps.

"Doing your homework, honey?" my mother asked softly.

"Yeah, I got a test tomorrow. I just can't get into studying."

She walked over to me. "Come here, Jason, let me feel your head."

"Mom, I'm fine."

"Are you coming down with something? You look like you're losing weight. How does your throat feel?"

I wanted to tell my mother what was going on, but I knew the trouble that would bring. Tender moments between us were rare. As irritated as I felt about her bothering me, I was also enjoying her concern.

"Mom, I'm just under a lot of stress right now. I have a test coming up. And a ton of homework building up."

"You're going to make yourself sick," she warned. "Those migraines will come back."

"Trust me, Mom, I'm fine. After this week everything will be more relaxed."

Sometime after, I decided it was time to show my parents some of Gacy's letters, a few that I picked because they made him seem pretty normal. Since my mother was a student of crime stories herself, I knew her curiosity would work to my advantage.

"Hey, Mom, check out this letter Gacy sent me. He's talking about what it's like in prison on Death Row."

At first, she seemed fascinated by the letters. Soon, though, the novelty wore off because the ones I selected for her to view were the most boring ones I could find.

"That's very interesting, Jason, but where are the *rest* of the letters? You know, the ones you lock away in your safe?"

Oops. I guess they knew more about what I was up to than I thought. The safe was a sore point between us. I'd been very concerned that my mother would start going through my stuff and discover what I was doing, so I purchased a large steel safe in which I could lock away my private things. It was handy for hiding not only my letters but also my collection of *Penthouse* and *Playboy* magazines.

"Mom," I tried to explain, although I could tell she wasn't believing me, "they all say the same things. We're like . . . well, we're just friends. I'm not going to show you all the letters because some of them are private to me."

After that, my parents stepped up their campaign to get me focused on something else. They nagged me constantly. They even teased me and called me gay. They'd ask at dinner, "Jason, are you still writing to your boyfriend in prison?" Then they'd laugh.

There was really little they could do, though. When I'm determined to do something, nothing can stop me. Still, I knew they were worried and they did their best to bring me back under control. The one thing I felt bad about is that I could hear my parents arguing all the time, Dad usually taking my side, telling Mom to leave me alone.

One of the consequences of having to be so secretive in my actions is that I became even more committed to following through on what I was doing. You can't imagine how inconvenient it was to leave school in the middle of the day to get the mail! The more time and energy I devoted to all this, the greater importance the letters began to have in my life. Each was like a trophy given to me by Gacy. It was like he was *validating* me, affirming me in a way that my parents rarely did. I actually felt grateful.

To be honest, I felt a kind of friendship. Remember, I wasn't corresponding with a man who talked about killing, or even sex all the time. Sometimes he'd ask about school, or we'd talk baseball and other sports.

Even when I asked him directly about the murders, he was convincing and logical in proclaiming his innocence. There were times when I'd actually believe what he was saying. He'd say, "Jason, so many other people had keys to my house. They were always coming and going. They were using drugs. I was working so many hours, I was never home. It was like my house was a recreation center for kids. I had a pool table and everything. Besides, do you really think I'm so stupid that I'd actually bury the bodies underneath my own house?"

He had a point.

Remember, too, that logic had always been my own favorite weapon—the tool I used to convince anyone of almost anything. Because I relied so much on logic myself, I was unusually susceptible to others' rational arguments. And I've got to tell you: Gacy was a master. Each time I'd poke a hole in his story, he'd find some way to explain it away. I was actually starting to feel more and more sympathetic to his cause—that is, until he changed the rules of our relationship.

13

Outside the Boundaries

In spite of all my efforts to choreograph the interactions between us, Gacy apparently had his own ideas about where we were headed. Judging by the content of his latest letter, he was prepared to play outside the boundaries I'd constructed.

"You mention you have a brother, 14," are the words that riveted my attention. "Is he into sports like you and do you get along with him?"

This might seem like the most ordinary of questions, but in hindsight, Gacy was planting seeds in the hope of acting out some very sick fantasies. I learned later through my correspondence with Gacy that he claimed to have had a youthful sexual relationship with his sister.

Since even in the best of circumstances I was overprotective of my brother, the red flags shot up soon after Gacy's first mention of Jarrod.

All the time my brother and I were growing up, both my parents worked long hours in retail and gaming jobs, so the responsibility often fell on me to be in charge. As much as I was plagued by my own fears, I was always even more concerned that something bad would happen to Jarrod.

I remembered the year before this whole serial killer project of mine started, Jarrod had gotten himself in a jam. He was a thirteen-year-old junior high schooler, while I was a senior in high school. Some gang members started bothering Jarrod, harassing him and following him around. One day they even put a dog chain around his neck and started choking him. A teacher arrived just in time to break things up.

When I heard what happened, I went berserk. My first impulse was to take care of the problem myself, find the kids and teach them a lesson. I was a big weight lifter and kickboxer at the time, so I had few doubts I could put the fear of God into them. But I didn't think that would be a long-term solution.

I presented Jarrod with my plan.

"Look, this whole situation could get totally out of hand. We don't want to deal with some gang war where someone will end up getting shot."

Jarrod listened intently. He was in over his head and anxious for a way out.

"If I kick this guy's ass," I explained, "then he'll just get someone bigger to kick both of our asses. I don't want this going back and forth forever."

"So what should we do?" he asked. I liked the sound of that "we"—this was our problem together and we'd solve it as a team.

"I'm going to take you to his house right now. Then you're going to fight him."

"Are you kidding?" he screamed. "He'll *kill* me."

"No he won't," I reassured him. "I'll make certain that doesn't happen. It'll be a fair fight."

Jarrod looked sick. Before he could think too much about it, I said, "Come on. Let's go."

"Right now?" he asked, taken completely off guard.

"Yes, Jarrod, right now. If you fight him at his house, then even if you kick his ass, he won't make a big deal of it because all his friends won't be there to get revenge."

All he could say in response was, "You want me to go right now?" He seemed to be in shock.

"Yeah, get your stuff and let's go. I won't let anything bad happen to you. I promise. If things get out of hand, I'll jump in."

Jarrod didn't look convinced.

"I know you're scared," I continued. "But you have to get this over with. Otherwise, this guy and his friends will never leave you alone. It's better that this asshole kicks your ass with me there than with all of his friends beating you with bats in the desert somewhere, leaving you for dead. We can end this whole thing today."

Jarrod trusted me completely, so he agreed to come. "If you say so, but if he starts kicking my ass too bad, you better break it up."

"Don't worry about it, Jarrod. You'll probably kick *his* ass!"

We went to the kid's house together and I set things up. "Here's the deal," I explained to the gangbanger, who was surprised by my offer. "You fight my brother right now. A fair fight. I'm tired of hearing all this bullshit about what you're doing to him at school. If you have a problem with Jarrod, then you can fight here like men, and I'll stand and watch. I won't do a thing, unless someone else steps in or you pull a knife or something. Then that's the end of it. If you beat the crap out of him, then leave him alone; if he beats you up, he leaves you alone. It's over."

"That's cool," he said, getting all pumped up at the idea of getting into a fight.

"Hey, man," I interrupted as he was pumping himself up, "I mean it. No matter what the hell happens, it ends here . . . *today*!"

"All right by me," he declared. "Let's get it on."

We all walked down the street to this deserted area where they were building new homes. Jarrod fought a good fight, but the guy was from the barrio in Los Angeles. He was tougher and had a lot more experience. Jarrod lost, ended up with a nice black eye, but he refused to give up. After that, he got a reputation for being one of the toughest kids in the school.

That was just one of several times when I came to Jarrod's defense, taking care of him when our parents were unavailable. Simply put, I tend to overreact whenever anyone tries to hurt my brother. Which is why I was more than a little concerned that Gacy was trying to bring him into this mess.

In the same letter that my brother's name was mentioned, Gacy also pressed for more communication between us. He challenged me to be more frank and open.

I am a PMA type person. Positive Mental Attitude. I don't have time for negative thinking. Death is negative so why fill your head with that. Lying is negative, so I have no time for that.

Hey, I say what I think to some. That's

great. To others, they think I am not tactful.
But I am not a cream puff and I believe a true
friend will not tell you what you want to hear
to stroke you but let you know whats right
from their point of view. So you won't find me
stroking you as you have your own hand for
that once a day if not more.

Again, there were those references to masturbation. And
also some tendentious comments, intended to paint a picture
of an upstanding man "caught up in the system." Gacy
would always preach to me about school, my grades, and
being good to my family. In his letters he mentioned everything from football scores to the new movies out on tape.
Clearly, these observations on pop culture were intended to
make me see him as a *person*, as no different than a friend
down the street.

A few days later I would receive my first glimpse of
what I'd learn to call the "artificial Gacy":

 . . . I did not kill or murder anyone. I owned
the property so they want you to assume I did.
They say I confessed, but have no confession
when asked in court. I have had 3 hours of
truth serum, showing that I had no knowledge
of some 28 victims, and the five I knew about,
it wasn't about killing them. That's not ad-
missible in court. I was sold out by my own
attorneys for book rights. Thats what I have
been appealing all of these years. But I am an
embarrassment on the criminal justice system,
because if I am right then they are wrong, and

too many careers and money have been made off
my name, and for political reasons its better
to kill me than to let the public know they
fucked up 15 years ago.

Although Gacy had included his "fact sheet" proclaiming
his innocence in the first letter he sent me, this self-serving
statement was consistent with what he would state over and
over again. At times, he was so persuasive I actually began
to believe him.

I'd heard about the so-called Stockholm syndrome in
which kidnap victims begin to identify with their captors to
the point where they feel sympathetic toward them, but I
never imagined that I'd come to feel something resembling
empathy for this cold-blooded murderer. I suppose, in retrospect, it was inevitable, but I was unprepared to deal with
the confusing feelings Gacy's letters evoked.

I wanted to look at this monster almost as a "speci-
men"—as a thing to be examined, analyzed, manipulated,
in some ways tested—yet I began to see him as a pitiful
human being who was doing the best he could like everyone else. I was repulsed by my own compassion. All I had
to do was think about Gacy's victims and their childless
parents to remember who and what I was really dealing
with.

14

Perversity

In my next letter to Gacy, I tried to lead him to an area in which he might begin to trust me more. In retrospect, I can't believe that I didn't anticipate the extent to which he would turn the tables back my way. The question I asked him was pretty direct: what he fantasized about sexually. I received a response six days later, just as my first semester of college was ending.

Gacy enjoyed being as graphic as possible in describing his sexual tastes. I realized this was another test of sorts, trying to determine my own preferences, as well as how I'd react to his explicit descriptions.

At first, I was sort of amused by what he wrote. I couldn't believe his lack of inhibition.

> What do I fantasize about sexually? I assume you mean when I jack off. Well, it depends on what mood I am in and what I am thinking from out of the many past encounters I have had. Since I like being the aggressor, I like to get on in threesomes. Both male and

female, making them my slaves in bed and doing
it all.

Straight sex or bi I enjoyed it all, knowing I can get off with both and enjoying anything that is consenting with others. I find
if you satisfy your partner first then you can
do anything. So I like to get them off first.

In talking about sex, I suspected that Gacy was unwittingly revealing his philosophy toward his victims as well.
As long as he helped them find satisfaction first, then he believed he had the right to do anything he wanted afterward,
up to and including torture and strangulation. I made a note
to follow up on this, to ask him at some future time what had
influenced him to let some boys go and others not.

In the letter, Gacy went on to explain that whereas he
hated homosexuals and "gay acting" people, he was actually bisexual—an orientation he considered quite natural.

He made a clear distinction between being with a man
for mutual pleasure and actually *loving* another man. He
thought that if there were no women around, then having
another guy to "get it on with" was the next best thing. Although he held this position until his death, before he was
arrested he'd completely stopped having sex with his wife
and slept only with males.

The word "consenting" in this letter was also something
that helped Gacy rationalize his actions and behavior. He
thought that as long as someone was consenting, then literally anything that ensued, sexually or physically, was okay.
This would hold equally true if the partner in question was
a handcuffed, fourteen-year-old boy who'd been handed an
ultimatum to perform oral sex on Gacy or die.

In my previous letter, I'd taken a bit of a risk by asking Gacy about the sense of power he felt when killing another human being—if indeed he'd actually killed anyone. Although he never stopped denying his guilt, he did slip innuendos into some of his correspondence referring to his crimes. This time, however, he chose to ignore my question about killing and instead talked about power in a sexual context.

> You asked about a sense of power. I think everyone feels that when having sex, be it with male or female. The power to bring someone off with your tongue is wild, as you have control over setting off their ejaculation, kind of like the power you have when beating it, you can bring it up and stop and hold off and then wait and bring it up again. Thats wild and to be honest with you I could even see doing it to you and having a lot of fun or even with you and your girlfriend getting both of you off without either of you touching the other.

> I loved wild parties. I think that when you have had an older woman you tend to want to control the younger one in doing what you want. What do you think? Older women like young toy boys as they call them. And its not the size of the ship, its the motion of the ocean. As anyone can fuck. Most like cut cocks circumcised. I am just 7" as I have been asked that many times, cut with a large head.

This portion of the letter struck me as significant in many ways. It was the first time he'd made any reference to involving me in one of his sexual ideas or thoughts. And he'd referred to me as a "toy boy," a term for a good-looking guy, sometimes a male prostitute, who gets what he wants by using his body.

In future letters, Gacy began addressing me as "toy boy," sometimes as an endearment, other times in a derogatory fashion. If I had any doubts that he was now thinking about me in a sexual way, his interest was confirmed when he asked for various photos of me posing in suggestive ways. Since there was a limit to what I'd do to keep him engaged, I merely sent him a few standard pictures.

He also brought up my brother again. "You mention your brother with no name or photo," he said. "I would think if your close then share that and give him a name. . . . Say hi to your brother tell him to stay with it [playing baseball], but enjoy life as well."

I was sitting on the porch one day, rereading these very words and reviewing other letters—much the way a miser savors his gold—when Jarrod arrived home from school. It was a perfect autumn day in the desert: cool, clear, bright sun. Jarrod had just gotten off the bus.

"Hey," I called out to him, "I want to talk to you about something."

"What did I do now?" he asked, only half joking. By my tone of voice, he thought he might be in trouble.

"Gacy has been asking about you," I said.

"What do you mean he's been asking about me?" he choked out.

"I think he has some sort of interest in you." For a moment, I wondered if I should have said anything. Jarrod looked sick.

"It might be innocent," I continued, "but I'm getting the impression he's going to want to get to know you better in the future."

"Jason," he begged, "please don't get me involved in this stuff. That guy's a freak. He *kills* people for a living!"

"Don't worry," I reassured him. "I've been thinking. What if I had you copy a letter to Gacy in your own handwriting so I—"

"No way. I'm not gonna—"

"Jarrod! Listen to me! You don't have to do anything except copy a letter I'm going to write. It needs to be in your handwriting. That's all you have to do. Nothing else."

"No way," he said, more firmly than I'd ever heard him.

I knew, though, that I could win him over if he'd just get into the spirit of the game.

"Listen to me," I pleaded. "I just want to play with him a little. If he thinks it's you writing, he'll tell you things he wouldn't tell me. It would give me two different sources of information I can cross-check."

Jarrod looked very skeptical but I could see he was listening.

"Besides," I said with a smile, "it'll be fun to fool him together."

I vowed to be very careful with Jarrod because I didn't want him to get hurt in any way. Such was my naiveté at the time that I figured I could control Gacy—send him like a rat through a maze in search of cheese. I thought of my brother as being like a silent partner, one with no real involvement or exposure.

Looking back on it, I think I was also partly in denial.

Already, just from having had limited contact with Gacy, my sleep had been disrupted, my schoolwork was suffering, and I was weighed down by secrets that left me feeling alone and isolated. By recruiting Jarrod, even in this limited role, I probably hoped to lessen the isolation.

I showed my brother just a few of Gacy's letters, ones that were free of the most blatant sexual references, especially anything related to homosexuality. It's amazing how many people assumed—then and later—that I must be gay to be able to play this role so authentically; I didn't want Jarrod to think that, too.

Once my brother signed on, I worked out a plan whereby I'd write Gacy two sets of letters, one from me, the other from my brother. I'd compose Jarrod's letters and then have him copy them in his own handwriting. Eventually, when the content of the letters flying back and forth became *really* weird, I told Jarrod to tell Gacy he was learning to type. That way, I could just do the letters myself on the computer and have Jarrod sign them without reading.

Of course, I never allowed Jarrod to read any of the letters sent directly to him. In fact, I wish that somebody else could have screened them so I wouldn't have had to read them either. But I have to admit: for a while, deceiving Gacy was sort of fun.

15

Fictional Friends

One afternoon I was sitting in the bleachers at the university softball field, watching the last half of the women's game with my friends. As usual, we were talking about which girls on the field were the "hottest" and bitching about our families.

"Man, I hate living at home," said my friend Randy.

"Yeah, me too," Josh added.

Randy continued, "I can't even bring my girlfriend home or my parents will give me shit for having someone in the house."

"Yeah," Josh agreed, "my mom is always on my ass."

Sitting there next to these guys I'd known for almost ten years, it occurred to me that they really knew less about me than Gacy did. There we were, watching girls running around in their skimpy outfits, and bullshitting with each other. Yet it felt like I had almost nothing in common with them.

I'd confided to Gacy not only some fabricated fantasies I thought he wanted to hear but also some very real feelings I had about life and the future. I'd shared with him my frustrations at home, my feelings of isolation, my hopes and aspirations. It felt weird to think that, in a strange way, he was actually becoming my *friend*.

At this point in our relationship, Gacy and I were relating to each other in a casual, relaxed manner. He was still feeling me out, testing what my limits were, and I was still trying to gauge how he viewed me, not knowing if he was as hesitant about me as I was about him.

I noticed one trend for certain: the more naive and confused I acted, the more confident and controlling Gacy became. It bolstered my opinion that he truly believed the character I was presenting was real.

In my letters to him, I'd taken great pains to present a family pattern that would seem very familiar to his own—I told him I had an overbearing mother and a very passive father. While this depiction was somewhat exaggerated, it was close enough to the truth to make me sound convincing.

Gacy frequently played psychologist, offering me his sage insights. In one letter, he observed:

> So it sounds like your dad is the passive
> one so maybe thats why you like to be domi-
> nated by older women. You ever think of that?
> I don't know the age of your parents but in
> the 40's your mother will go through a change
> of life so maybe thats what is happening now.
> Just be kind to her. Your dad has the right
> idea of just being passive.

I fabricated a family situation in which I was suffering abuse at the hands of my parents, both emotionally and physically. Attempting to echo as strongly as possible Gacy's own background, I blamed this on the weakness of my father. Likewise, I invented scenarios in which my father had beaten me in much the same way I knew Gacy had been mistreated. I figured: if Gacy is able to relate to my suffering, he might give me insight into how these situations affected him. The other reason for spinning these tales was that it created an impression I could shortly be homeless— banished by either my father's or my own decision. I suspected that Gacy would seize on this as an opportunity to instruct me in novel ways to earn money. And he didn't disappoint.

He coached me on how to sell myself on the streets and how to make my body my most important tool. He described how interested "buyers" would act and how I should act with them. Basically, he was giving me a tutorial in how to be the perfect victim.

Although he claimed sympathy for my abusive situation, he insisted that being passive was a good quality. The fact is, he *wanted* me to become overwhelmed by those who were strong and could break me down. Right from the beginning, he set the tone for me to enter the world of submission to his authority. Key to this was getting me to see that being passive, or even humiliated, was okay—that sometimes it was necessary.

Of course, many of my hypotheses, assumptions, analyses, and explanations as to what happened and why were formulated after the events occurred. I wasn't operating quite as deliberately and systematically as it might seem.

I did have a general plan, but it wasn't nearly as well developed as it now might sound, with the luxury of years to reflect on my behavior. While it's true that I spent hundreds of hours analyzing every word Gacy sent me, and every word I sent back, I sometimes wasn't fully conscious of what I was doing.

Years later, after taking a dozen psychology courses, reading everything ever written on the subject of serial killers, consulting with the FBI, doing an internship with the U.S. Secret Service, and writing an honors thesis on this experience, *then* I could look back on what happened with some clarity. At the time Gacy and I were exchanging letters, though, I was mostly shooting from the hip, trying things out, experimenting to see what would work even if I couldn't exactly explain why.

Sex is what Gacy wanted to talk about in every letter. He continuously interrogated me about my own experiences, trying to get a handle on what my inclinations were so he could determine the best way to play me. At first, I found his perversity disgusting. But after a while, I stopped dwelling on the images and viewed his off-the-wall approaches as, well, like a chess game or a mathematical problem to solve. *If he says this, I should say that.*

Since he kept badgering me to tell him about what I'd done previously, the first fantasy I offered up was one I could easily relate to: being seduced by an older woman. I knew that he'd had a similar experience in his youth, the difference being that his was with an older *man.* Even so, the similarity between the two experiences seemed likely to forge a point of connection. When I actually sat down at my desk to construct the scenario, I smiled with satisfaction as I thought about a twist in the story I could create—one that would feed Gacy's obsession with bisexuality. The excerpt from my letter reads as follows:

One night I was at a Christmas party and this pretty woman came up and started talking to me. The conversation went well, and we decided to go into a room of the house where we could have some privacy. One thing led to another and we started kissing passionately. I asked her if I could go down on her, and she said yes. After working my way up her thighs she pulled away, and stopped me. She then laid me down on the bed and performed oral sex on me, and gave me the best orgasm of my life. I was very happy with her. After a few minutes, she told me she was a man, a transvestite, and if I was still interested I could call her the next day. I never called her again.

Saying a prayer that my parents and friends would never stumble across this balderdash, I told Gacy I was very excited about the whole incident—that it prompted me to masturbate for the next three days. While I didn't say explicitly that it was the woman's true gender that got me all hot and bothered, the message was clear.

I'd studied Gacy's ideas about sexuality at length and knew he was in great denial about his homosexuality. Like so many serial killers, he was the type of person who tries to destroy in others the part of himself he most wishes to disown. His theory was that everyone is bisexual and wants to act on those tendencies, given the opportunity. He also believed that most older men are inclined to seduce younger ones, whether they're enlightened enough to do so or not.

Since Gacy considered me attractive, he assumed men

were hitting on me daily. I came to realize that some of the places where he thought I *should* have been approached were actually ones where he'd begun to fantasize I'd *be* approached. "Never been hit on being in sports?" he asked me. "That's hard to believe."

Gacy believed it was virtually impossible for me to have played sports for so many years and not have been seduced by a coach or a parent. I eventually concluded that, if I didn't come up with a story regarding a seduction during my athletic career, my overall credibility would be in doubt.

It seemed clear that, after having spent fourteen years in prison, Gacy was even more sadistic, perverse, and sexually driven than before he arrived. Even in his fifties, he appeared to be more dangerous and aggressive than ever. Without a way to vent his twisted desires, the pressure of his fantasies was building to extreme levels.

He wanted me to see how innocent and natural homosexual encounters actually were. In his letter of December 28, 1993, he described his first *voluntary* experience since being sexually abused as a child.

Regarding my first encounter, I was 22. He and I went to dinner after work. His conversation was about sex, I assume feeling me out. He said that when he goes out he has a 100% chance of finding something while I only have 50%. I asked him to explain. He said if I went out and couldn't find a female then I would go home and jack it off, whereas with him if he doesn't find a female, he finds a guy to get him off.

Then the drinks came faster and by the time we left I was high, but I drove him to his place. He asked me in for coffee, instead we had another drink or two. I passed out on the sofa, but awoke like in a dream with something wet down between my legs. In the dark room I could see his head, but didn't move as he had all seven inches in his warm wet mouth going up and down and under the crown of my cut head.

He seemed to know all the right spots as he had me lifting my hips as I fed his mouth until it went off like a firecracker, and flooded his mouth, and dripped from the sides. He continued to lick it clean, returned my pants up and went off to bed. I awoke in the morning never saying a word. Had coffee and went home and took a shower and jacked it off again. Never has any girls gotten me off as well. It was nearly a year before I encountered it again and then it was mutual and while drinking. But that's an excuse anyway just like your doing it with a TV [transvestite] even not knowing you liked it and that's all that counts.

Besides the obvious—Gacy's fondness for graphic sexual imagery—the other thing that struck me about this letter and others that followed was that they were grammatical disasters. Despite his background—Gacy had been a well-off community leader prior to being incarcerated—he churned out pages of botched prose that showed him to be basically uneducated. It was yet another example of his presenting a certain face to the world while being something else entirely.

Before signing off, Gacy mentioned something that would change the course of our relationship from that point onward. He jokingly wrote, "Too bad you don't have a phone, as I could call collect sometime where you can ask your questions during the story. Ha ha."

I thought to myself, *Wow! This is incredible! The guy wants to talk to me on the phone.* I couldn't believe my luck. If I could get this much out of him via letter writing, what could I do using a phone! Of course, the thought of actually speaking to someone like this—where I'd truly have to act out the role I was playing—caused some trepidation, but the novelty value alone was too high to pass up. How many people could say they received phone calls from a serial killer?

Gathering up my courage, I wrote Gacy back, giving him the number of my personal phone line, whose only extension was in my room. I told him the best time to reach me was on Sundays.

For a while after sending the letter, I worried what I'd say if my parents got wind of this. I could just imagine my brother answering the phone in my room and yelling throughout the house: "Jason. Telephone. It's for you. John Wayne Gacy, the serial killer, is on the phone. He's calling collect from Death Row."

There was also the problem of paying for the calls. They'd be collect, since inmates can't make regular calls. My parents, especially my father, were very concerned about money—mostly because they've never had much. I knew there was no way they'd let me accept a collect call from anyone, unless we were reimbursed.

Still, I decided to deal with those problems if and when they arose. As it turned out, my next few communications from Gacy were in letter form. At one point in my previous correspondence, I'd asked him directly if he was attracted to me, hoping to catch him off guard. Now he said that I was too inhibited for him as a partner, but he admitted that he fantasized "getting it on" with me, especially if I was interested in having an "older teacher."

As I would later learn, my tossing out that "attraction" question gave Gacy the green light to bring up the subject anytime he liked. It was as if he'd never thought of me as a sexual object before this query came his way, but since it had . . .

Gacy, like most sociopaths, would never take responsibility for his actions, and could manipulate any situation to portray himself as the victim. To him, I was the one who caused him to see me in a sexual way; he'd never considered such a thing prior to my bringing it up.

In one of his subsequent letters, he took the opportunity to present me with a brief analysis of my own personality, as well as the reasons why I was writing him in the first place.

> You can't tell another what to do as life
> is experiences. It depends how open you are.
> Your still learning so who is to say how far
> to go, and if you could be unselfish and giv-
> ing as well as receiving without hang ups. I
> think you want to. I also think you wrote me
> because it was a male sexual case, and you
> thought you could learn from me. That's fine,
> but your like asking me to give you the green

light of approval when I know you want to anyway. Hey go for it. If you were here around me
you would try it all, then decide. We all control ourself.

I had a number of reactions to this analysis. First, I was
pleased that he thought me so transparent and that he'd apparently been taken in completely by the role I was playing.
Second, I was a bit unnerved to realize he was right about
my wanting his approval, although not in the way he imagined.

The fact is Gacy had become an important person in my
life. If nothing else, he was a source of status among my
friends. But he was also, I'll admit, a bit of an addiction.
Like a Sunday golfer who practices his swing throughout
the week, dreaming of getting out there on the links, I found
myself constantly daydreaming about how I'd parry Gacy's
latest prying question, or elicit from him another nugget of
insight.

By now I was feeling confident enough that I decided to
test his connection to me. In my next letter to him, I acted
furious at his misinterpretation of my motives. I told him
that all I wanted was friendship and that maybe I shouldn't
continue writing him if he thought I had some ulterior motive. I told him that, although I *had* discussed sexual things
with him occasionally in my letters, sex, and anything related to sex, was the last thing I was interested in.

This response completely floored Gacy. Now he was
confused about what I was really searching for in our relationship. For the moment, I felt like I was the one in control. I figured he needed me more than I needed him, and
that he'd have to invest even more in the relationship.

16

What's Up, Buddy?

his is a collect call from inmate . . . 'John Gacy' . . . from the Menard Correctional Center. To accept the call, say yes after the tone."

It was nine o'clock on a Sunday morning when the phone rang. I was sound asleep when I grabbed—or rather knocked—the receiver off the hook, struggling to think clearly. Rather than a live person, I heard an unearthly recorded, mechanical voice speaking without inflection.

"Huh?" I muttered into the receiver, realizing as I said it that I wasn't selecting one of the offered choices.

I was now fully awake. In fact, I could never recall feeling more alive than at that moment. "Yes," I said softly, and then much louder: "Yes, operator, I accept. I mean, I'll accept the call." What an idiot I sounded like, but before I could berate myself further, I heard a real voice, a human voice.

"What's up, buddy?"

Silence from me. I was utterly speechless, unable to form a single word. I just sat up in bed, mute, gripping the phone in a tight clinch, trying to organize my thoughts and remind myself to stay in role. I kept telling myself to stay calm, that I could do this, that I could be a good actor when I wanted to be. There was, however, another voice in my head simultaneously saying, "Jason, this is John Wayne Gacy, one of the most successful killers in the country. His full attention is now directed toward *you*."

"I know this is probably awkward for you," Gacy tried to reassure me. "Just relax. I'm watching TV right now, just hanging out in my cell. What about you?"

I felt so nervous, I still couldn't respond immediately. "Uh, sorry. I was out late last night. I just woke up."

"Out late banging your girlfriend?" Gacy asked with a snicker.

Another long pause while I tried to gather my thoughts and figure out where this was going. "Yeah," I played along. Then I tried to change the subject. "I can't believe I'm actually talking to you." I hoped I sounded appropriately passive and helpless like my chosen character. The fact is, at that point I did feel pretty helpless.

Gacy immediately began talking about the letter I'd just sent him in which I'd sounded hurt and angry. "Don't worry about the letter," he said, his voice conciliatory. "You're taking it way too seriously. I didn't mean that you were trying to use me or anything. It's just that so many people write because of that reason."

"Yeah, well, I'm not one of those people," I told him, trying to sound firm in my own way.

"I didn't say that you were. I apologize for how it sounded in the letter. You just don't understand how many people want something from me. I really didn't mean that you're like that. Don't worry, bud, okay?"

All the while Gacy was apologizing to me, I couldn't

keep from grinning. He really did believe I was who I pretended to be. He was doing everything he could to ingratiate himself, to make amends. I wiped the pleased smile off my face to remain consistent with my character. I remembered that I was supposed to be feeling indignant.

"John, what you wrote in your letter was complete bullshit! None of that was true, you know!"

Saying this to Gacy was probably the hardest thing I'd ever done in my life. No matter how many times I told myself that he was only on the phone, thousands of miles away, I still thought that if I went too far with my act, he'd somehow find a way to get me, just like those monsters in the movies.

I held my breath as I waited to see how he'd respond. It seemed like hours before he said anything. I could almost feel him thinking on the other end of the line, making his own calculations.

"You can be a feisty little shit, can't you?" he replied in a tone of voice that was starting to irritate me. "What's the matter, Jason? Didn't you get enough sex last night?" He started laughing at his feeble attempt to change the subject.

"John, I'm being serious. I really think we're going to have problems if you think I'm some freak writing you because I need sexual advice."

What I found most disconcerting about this conversation was that it was like we were lovers who'd had an argument and were trying to make up. I was stuck in the role of the victim and was pretending to act hurt, while he was playing a part of his own, pretending he was sorry for his insensitivity. As exciting as all this was, I also couldn't help but feel disgusted that I was acting like such a wimp.

From the literature I'd read, I knew Gacy was running

true to form. It was his habit, I knew, with those who would eventually become his victims, to settle disputes by offering a gift or a pay raise, accompanied by an earnest expression of remorse and a promise he'd never do it again. Of course, within hours or days he'd break his word—sometimes in the most vile and lethal way possible.

"Jason, how 'bout if I send you one of my paintings? I've got this one called *Pennywise the Clown*. It's from Stephen King's book *It*. It looks really nice. It's one of the most requested pieces that I paint. One just like it sold in a New York art gallery for $10,000."

"Yeah, that would be great," I answered him much more calmly than I felt. Actually, I was screaming inside my head. I couldn't believe it! I knew Gacy had taken up painting in prison, doing mostly ghoulish portraits of clowns and other subjects. While they weren't great works of art, he did have a certain demented flair, and his signature at the bottom made them valuable.

After some more awkward conversation, I tried to end the call, but he was determined to keep me on the line as long as he could. "Hey, John," I finally told him, "my mom's calling me. I really have to go now."

The truth of the matter was that I'd coped with about as much of him as I could stand. I needed some time to regain my composure, to catch my breath.

"All right, then, I've got a lot of shit to do, too." *Oh yeah?* I wondered what he could possibly be talking about. He *was* locked up in a prison cell all day, wasn't he?

He threw out one more line, just to keep me talking. "Did you ever see that interview where I was on *Hard Copy*?"

I admitted I had. It was about the paintings he'd done of Adolf Hitler. I wondered why he was bringing that up now. He knew I was Jewish. Still, I couldn't deal with any more mind games. I needed time to digest what had already happened.

"Okay, I'll be right there," I screamed off into space, as if I was answering my mother. "John, I really have to go now. My mom is going to kill me if I don't get downstairs."

"Yeah. All right. I gotta go, too. Just keep them letters coming. I'll talk to you again real soon." *Click.*

I was shaking. I'd held it together. I actually managed to talk to John Wayne Gacy, pretending to be his friend. Maybe I was going to get away with this after all.

While I was mulling over whom I could possibly share this experience with without their thinking me a freak, the phone rang again. I calmly picked it up to discover it was another collect call request. My heart stopped. Why was he calling again? What did he want? I could only imagine the worst.

"How are ya?" he came on, like we hadn't just gone through this ten minutes ago. My heart was pounding. With a barely disguised sense of dread, I said, "Fine. What's up, John?"

"I was just calling you back because I didn't think you'd believe it was me who called. I wanted to let you know it was really me."

Again, I was speechless. I had no idea what he was up to or how to respond. I felt a big headache coming on.

He continued on, pretending the lengthy silence wasn't really as awkward as it felt. "Well, I guess I'll let you go now. Remember to keep the letters coming."

There was another pause. Then: "Are you going to tell your family I called?"

"Well, maybe," I said, stalling for time. I wasn't sure what he wanted me to say. I figured it was best if he thought I wasn't that close to my parents.

"Well, send them my regards. Talk to ya soon, buddy."

As I hung up the phone, I realized the implications of what had just occurred. Gacy was obviously interested in a very intimate, intense relationship. Furthermore, he was impatient to move as quickly as possible. Of course, that made perfect sense when you considered he was sentenced to die in just a few months; he didn't have a lot of time to waste.

Bursting with too much excitement to keep it bottled up, I ran downstairs to find Jarrod and my mother eating breakfast.

"Hey, guess what? Guess who I was just talking to?" They could tell something was up.

"Gacy," I blurted out. "He actually called. Can you guys fuckin' believe it!"

"Watch your mouth," my mother reminded.

"No way!" my brother gasped. "Are you serious?" His fork, which had been en route to his mouth, now clattered to the table.

It was obvious my mother didn't think I was serious. "Sure he called," she said sarcastically. Then, as if I didn't know the rudimentary facts of life, she added, "They can't make calls from prison."

"Yes they can," I answered. "They can only use the phone on certain days, but they can call anyone they want."

"Jason, you're definitely sick," my mother responded.

"I can't believe you had this guy call our house. This is definitely getting out of hand."

"I never really thought he'd do it," I said, defending myself with a half-truth. "God, this makes everything I'm doing so real. I can't believe I actually talked to this guy on the phone."

"This is too weird," my brother said. Anticipating a blowup between my mother and me, he left the room.

"Who do you think is going to pay this phone bill?" my mother said, closing in for the kill. "*We* sure the hell aren't. You better get yourself a job." In a huff, she began cleaning up the dishes from the night before.

"Mom," I said with more than a little exasperation, "why are you so concerned about stuff like that? Don't you realize who I was just on the phone with? John Wayne Gacy. The serial killer!"

My mother was unimpressed, or at the very least, she was determined not to *seem* impressed. She simply refused to talk about it, except to mention the money: "If Gacy is willing to pay for it, then fine. I just think that what you've got yourself involved in is ridiculous."

That's the last time I would tell my parents much about what I was up to. I'd make sure they received all the checks Gacy eventually sent to cover the phone calls, but beyond that, it was information blackout. Whatever I was going to do, I'd have to do it on my own, with only a little support from my brother.

I spent the rest of the day talking to Jarrod about the phone conversation I had with Gacy. My brother seemed impressed that I'd been able to keep my cool. But he was also worried: "Look, I don't want you to think I'm a pussy or anything, but I'm not going to answer your phone anymore. It could be him calling and I don't want to even hear his voice."

I later learned that this was when Jarrod began having terrible nightmares that would disrupt his sleep for weeks at a time. My own would soon follow.

17

A Back Door

I received a letter from Gacy the next day, obviously mailed before we'd talked on the phone. From this point forward, he kept an almost constant stream of mail coming to my house, often three or four letters per week. He sent packages as well, one including the painting he'd promised me, others filled with pornographic books and photos of nude men.

In addition to the increased presence of sexual fantasies in his letters, there was also a certain egomania. Again and again he touted his "accomplishments" to demonstrate his superiority over me. One letter reminded:

> Much of what is known about me is slanted
> from a media point of view so as time goes on
> I will try to explain fact from fiction. Keep
> in mind there are 11 hard bound books out on
> me, 42 others with full chapters on me, two
> screen plays, one movie, one off Broadway
> play, 5 songs written about me, and over 500

articles on me. And 80% of them are fantasy
and fraud.

As absurd as this "list of credits" was, there was also
something remarkable about it. Here was this stone-cold
killer—just an old, fat man sitting in prison, whose one dis-
tinguishing trait was a willingness to take lives without remorse—and yet he had the whole world clamoring at his
feet, including me. Something was wrong here.

Such was the intensity of the spotlight that shone on
Gacy that he forgot at times that it was his *crimes* that had
made him famous. Rather, he convinced himself that it was
the force of his personality or his intellect that had won him
all this attention. Even though he was about to die for his
actions, I don't think he ever had a single regret. He absolutely loved the attention he was getting, the hundreds of
requests for interviews, and all the fan mail.

Eventually, I would learn that, even though he was stuck
in prison, he still managed to live like a celebrity. He had a
private cell, a television set, money to spend from the sale
of his paintings, and guards eating out of his hands, willing
to do almost anything for him. He'd even alleged that he
met with the warden a few times each month to extract various privileges. Such was his regal status.

After wading through pages thick with braggadocio, it
was almost a relief to see Gacy return to his favorite subject: kinky sex. *Almost* a relief.

One of Gacy's obsessions was a form of masturbation
called "head-over-head." It consisted of lying on the ground
and leaning one's butt against a wall in such a way that the
hips (or as Gacy would prefer, the head of one's penis) were
higher than one's head. Once in this position, the masturba-

tor would then proceed to stroke himself, and when an orgasm was achieved, the semen would discharge all over his face.

He spoke about this technique a lot, although he claimed that because of his weight and age, he could no longer practice it. He was insistent, though, that I give it a try—obviously because it was one of his favorite fantasies of what he wanted to do to me. Since he couldn't be physically present, he wanted me to act out both roles. I also realized that, in a way, he was *training* me. Since I'd admitted to him that I hadn't yet had a homosexual encounter, he was preparing me, little by little, to move in that direction.

After I confirmed—in the face of relentless hounding—that I'd at last given his special recipe a try (I'd done no such thing), Gacy soon let up on the subject and assumed I was "head-over-heading" on a regular basis. Every now and again he'd ask about my most recent "self-loving" encounter, and I'd make up a new story, logging it in a journal with the date so I wouldn't forget what I'd said.

After he and I began speaking on the phone, the letters took a different turn. They now became supplements to our conversations, which would often last for an hour or more every Saturday and Sunday morning and sometimes even occur midweek.

Partly, my willingness to spend that much time talking to Gacy was attributable to the boredom I experienced as a college student living at home. Partly, it was a testament to his ability to adroitly shift gears from luridly entertaining to supportive, depending on my mood.

Gacy always sculpted his letters in such a way that they'd be specific and unique to each person, yet disguise his own wrongdoing. This became even more true once the phone relationship commenced.

At first, I didn't understand why he'd care what anyone thought. After all, he'd already been convicted of murder and was waiting for his execution. He'd exhausted all of his appeals. What else did he have to lose? As it turned out, though, he actually believed that someone—a judge, a Supreme Court justice, the governor of Illinois, even the president—would eventually commute his sentence. He'd vowed to be very careful, since he believed his behavior would be subjected to close scrutiny.

One of his tactics was to use code words—to disguise people's names, incidents that had occurred, or things he wanted me to do. Though he told me he was using the words to protect my privacy, they were there to cover his tracks if anything went wrong.

"Look, Buddy," he explained, "if we talk about some stuff on the phone that's unique or about something you're into, when I write you next I'll say something like 'How's the project?' That way, your parents won't get upset if they find one of your letters." He was always positioning himself as someone who was looking out for my best interests.

Because part of me knew that he was trying very hard to manipulate me, I felt less guilty manipulating him. I suppose I shouldn't have felt guilty at all. One could make the argument that Gacy, as someone who'd brutally killed thirty-three men and boys, wasn't entitled to honesty or fair play. But such virtues were sufficiently ingrained in me that it was sometimes difficult to keep up the deception.

In the end, a part of me realized that if I *didn't* deceive him, the relationship would yield nothing positive. Direct questioning was not the route to go with Gacy.

I knew, for example, that if I asked him, "How did you feel and react to your father beating you?" I'd get nowhere. That's the usual approach taken by psychologists who interview serial killers, and it yields little useful information because there's no way you can trust the answers given. Gacy had probably been asked that question a hundred times, and if I asked it for the 101st time, I'd get the response he gave everyone else.

I figured it would be more productive to concoct a personal situation that he could offer his opinion on. So during one phone conversation, I batted away yet another question about my sex life and adjusted my actor's hat.

"John, I don't want to talk about that stuff right now. I'm really fuckin' pissed off." My voice cracked, adding the proper authenticity. "I told you my father was giving me some shit again. I just want to die," I said, seemingly on the verge of tears.

"Jason, you need to calm down. Now, why do you want to die?"

"My dad beat my ass again last night. He fuckin' threw me against the wall and my head smacked into this nail. I hate that asshole. I really hate that fucker."

"Jason, you don't hate anyone," Gacy replied in his most soothing voice. If I didn't know better, I'd think it was a "TV dad"—*The Brady Bunch*'s Mike Brady? *The Cosby Show*'s Dr. Huxtable?—on the other end of the line.

"Fuck that, John," I replied, starting to feel pretty bold at this point. I waited, hoping he'd catch the drift of where I was heading.

"Jason, just relax," he finally responded. "The same thing happened to me. My father would smack the hell out of me for no reason at all. They love you, but sometimes they get angry. Once my dad hit me so hard over the head with a broomstick that I opened my eyes and found myself being held by my mother. I forgave him, just like you'll forgive your dad."

"But, John, it's worse for me. I'm not sure I even want to live anymore. I have nobody. I can't trust anyone. I can't talk to anyone. It's just . . . you know . . ."

"Yeah, yeah," Gacy jumped in. "I know what you're going through. My old man never even told me he loved me. Sure, there were times I wanted to kill myself, but if you die, then they are the ones who'll win."

His voice was now getting very serious and low. "I learned to turn all my anger inwards. Jason, you'll soon learn how to not let people like that get to you. There are other ways to handle those situations."

I was shocked at the direction this conversation was taking. If I wasn't mistaken, Gacy was actually telling me about how he'd learned to strike out at others for all the abuse he'd suffered as a child.

He continued, "I'm here for you, Jason. I'm your friend. Your *only* friend. The only friend you need. Right now you need your parents because you have nowhere else to live. Keep hustlin' and the money will be rollin' in and you can move out. Maybe I could help out in the future, too."

I couldn't believe it. He was getting really emotional about all this. It almost seemed as if I'd opened a back door to his psyche, gained access to emotions he hadn't expressed in a long time, if ever.

He went on to confide that he'd thought many times about killing himself, especially when, in the midst of serving a prison sentence—his first—for rape, he learned his father had died.

"Jason, the Bible preaches against taking your own life, but sometimes it's the right thing to do. Your life will hit rock bottom someday, and when the time is right, you'll know what to do, and also how to do it."

Was he telling me there'd come a time when he wanted me to kill myself, maybe after his execution? Or maybe he was admitting his plan to take his own life before the state could do it. Either way, I couldn't get his words out of my mind.

18

Incest

Just when I thought there was nothing new that Gacy could surprise me with, he brought up an idea on the phone that broke new ground: he wanted me to have an incestuous relationship with my brother! The notion of a homosexual encounter was, to me, distasteful enough—but sex with *Jarrod*? It was beyond sick.

I tried to change the subject immediately, redirecting things toward a safer area. But Gacy could be persistent. In the past, he'd suggested I have sex with friends, my mom— even my dog! But my "doing it" with Jarrod—the image drove him crazy.

So obsessed was he by this notion that I eventually decided something might be learned by appearing to entertain it.

During our next phone conversation, I acted stupid for not considering the possibility of sex with my brother sooner. It was natural I'd show reluctance, and this only stimulated him to increase the intensity of his sales pitch. As he methodically ticked off the reasons for sibling sex, he sounded like a spokesman for H&R Block.

"You *need* to get off, Jason. I know your girlfriend is not giving it to you every day," he said.

"You're right, John."

"You know guys can get you off just as well as girls. We've gone over this before."

Still acting very hesitant, I mumbled back, "Yeah, I guess."

He continued pressing. "Your brother isn't gettin' any either. Don't you see what a waste this is? Why hold out when you guys have each other? You and your brother can trust one another completely. It's safe, clean, and discreet. Hell, why not get him off a couple of times until he keeps coming back for more?"

As I listened without responding, he said, "You don't know how lucky you are to be in the situation you're in."

"What do you mean?"

"You guys can use each other to get off all day long. At night. In the morning. All day long."

"I don't know," I said. "It just doesn't sound right. If my parents found out, I'd be thrown out of the house for sure. I'd have nowhere to go."

"Relax, Jason. Nobody will ever find out. Just slide into his bed at night, or in the morning, and start wrestling around with him until you get him hard. After a while, he'll get used to it, then just let your head end up in his crotch and just take it in your mouth. He might get nervous at first, but then he'll begin to get into it and let you finish the job. After you get him off once, then he'll be yours. If he gives you any trouble after that, you can just remind him: 'So, I was good enough to blow you once, but now it's not okay?' "

"I guess" were the only words that I could get out of my

mouth at this point. I wasn't sure how much more of this conversation I could handle.

Eventually, I learned to distract myself during Gacy's sicker tangents. Sometimes, while he was talking, I'd read a magazine; sometimes I'd watch the television with the sound down low; sometimes I'd jot down notes.

But at this point I was meeting his prurience head-on, and it was tough to take.

"Call Jarrod into your room right now," Gacy said, hoping to close the sale.

"Okay, hold on a second." After leaving him hanging for a minute, I acted disappointed because, unfortunately, "Jarrod had baseball practice early in the morning and he still isn't home yet."

"Oh well. Just make sure and try this afternoon or tonight when he gets home."

Yeah, *right*.

A few days later, Gacy mailed me a letter in which he elaborated on how I should go about seducing my brother:

> Regarding J [the code he assigned to Jarrod] and experiencing that, well the best way is to get into conversation and find out how open his thinking is. At that age anyone is horny and its better then getting off by hand. But its not much the doing as the feeling you will get from the other that you never knew you had.
>
> I would think the best way is show by example meaning your going to be the one catching and then they get the feeling that if its good enough for you they don't feel embarrassed.

But you have a perfect partner since you share
the other things and he looks to you as his
mentor. The other sensations will be letting
him think he is controlling you while your
doing the leading. The sensation also of taking not only oral but letting ride the back
door. I have known some who got off in a wild
way just having someone do them. But you have
to feel out his thinking and if he is willing
to experiment. If that is a green light the
next move is being aggressor to show him that
you were serious, or he will think it was just
a joke. That age it will be a sweet load of
adventure and way of trying new things and
will draw you closer in a way.

He went on to describe in detail how I should sneak into
Jarrod's room at night and how I should handle any resistance I might encounter. He supplied some rationalizations I
could use to justify this seduction—chief among them, that
we were only masturbating together, giving each other pleasure. The part that fascinated me the most, though, was that,
unwittingly, he was actually training me in the techniques he
used to seduce and control his victims.

In Gacy's intense tutoring sessions on how I could seduce my brother, he made it clear that these same strategies
had been tested previously on very young boys. He gave me
a rundown of every scenario that could possibly occur. He
went into detail on how to respond to my brother—or anyone—who might get apprehensive about engaging in sexual
acts. He described strategies for how to reassure no matter
what the response. He had an answer for all occasions.

In his very next letter, he attempted to normalize this type of sexual relationship by maintaining that he had had a sexual relationship with his sister when they were children. To the best of my knowledge, this was the first time he'd actually claimed to sibling incest. While the following scenario could have been a fantasy, or at least an embellishment, I'm convinced that something emotional lay at the heart of it—maybe merely an unrequited sexual love for a person he couldn't possess.

> She and I were in separate rooms, but it never stopped us from having some pleasure. But while she was unsure about it, I had to be the aggressor making the late night trips. I would already be down to just my bikini briefs, and would slip into her room and just slide in.
>
> Just as soon as she knew I was there I would tell her to be quiet. As I move my hand over her nipples, until they were hard, then I would move down rubbing her until she was getting wet and slipped my hand inside making her become aroused. Once that was done I would slip down and let my tongue do the work, until she got off at least once. I did this a couple of times without any return favor, just to show her it was safe. Later I would get her going and then move into a 69, and then it took off by itself after a couple times.

The amount of personal information that was now flowing from Gacy was immense. So far, our correspondence and phone conversations had yielded enough intriguing detail that I couldn't help daydreaming about what might be gleaned from other serial killers.

If I could get to Gacy, what about Charles Manson, Richard Ramirez, Henry Lee Lucas, David Berkowitz, and Elmer Wayne Henley, Jr.? Or even Jeffrey Dahmer?

I was flying so high I believed anything was possible.

THE LAST VICTIM 119

19

Joining a Family

Although I was swollen with overconfidence, I did feel a certain amount of anxiety reaching out to serial killers who struck me as even *more* diabolical than Gacy, if only because their behavior was more inscrutable. There was something about Gacy that seemed *predictable*. His neuroses were categorizable, his method of selecting victims fairly clear. But what about a madman like Charles Manson? There's no way anyone could make much sense of what *he* might do next. Perhaps because of the challenge inherent in that, I selected him as the next killer to contact.

My research revealed that Charles Manson was the leader of a drug-crazed gang of male and female hippies who were known as "the family." They were convicted of nine murders, all without apparent motive. Included in their killing spree was Hollywood film star Sharon Tate, who, while pregnant, was slowly tortured and stabbed dozens of times. Also murdered were four friends and a servant. One particularly chilling aspect of this crime was the way the killers scribbled the words "helter skelter" on the wall in the victims' blood.

Manson and seven members of his gang were sentenced to death in 1972. These sentences were commuted to life imprisonment a year later when the California Supreme Court voted to abolish the death penalty. Since his conviction, Manson has been a permanent resident of the California prison system, making news every time he comes up for parole.

Even with Manson locked away, his reign of terror continued for some time afterward. Several members of his "family" were ordered executed after his conviction. His own defense attorney was found murdered after the guilty verdict came in. Most notably, Lynette "Squeaky" Fromme, one of Manson's followers, attempted to assassinate President Gerald Ford, but her pistol misfired.

Manson fascinated me for a number of reasons. First, he represented the ultimate in what people fear the most: a violent, angry, unpredictable man who'll not only kill on the slightest whim but can convince others to kill for him as well. Also part of the profile: a certain randomness or irrationality to victim selection. Anyone can be a target, though in Manson's case it helped if he perceived you to be an annoyance or part of "the establishment."

When I watched Manson on television, he came across as a crazy extremist. He seemed incoherent at times—often, he just didn't make much sense. I couldn't help wondering how much of this was real and how much an act. There was a part of him that seemed very calm, very calculating. And at one point in his life, he'd been persuasive enough to get a group of young people to do anything he asked. On balance, there seemed more there than met the eye.

I surmised that the best way to get Manson to look my way was to show that I respected him—that I was, in a sense, a "colleague" interested in furthering his mission. I would present myself as his ideal follower in the same way I presented myself to Gacy as his ideal victim. I assumed Manson still wanted people on the outside continuing his "work."

In my first letter to the famous cult leader, I constructed a carefully worded request to join his family:

Dear Charles,

I decided to write you this letter because I was told that we have very similar philosophies on life and society by a mutual friend, John Solders, who lives in NY. He told me that you were a very powerful man, and that together we could solve a common goal, fixing all the fucking problems with society.

Ya know, I am now starting to understand why the white man is starting to fall. There is a big powerful hole in society which needs to be filled. The scum are out there, and there is nothing we can do about it; at least there is nothing that I can do about it. You are the one with a plan. You have the vision that could save us all. I would really appreciate you teaching me the way to save the man. I want to save the children and the women, and I want to save you.

You have done so much for the cause, and I can continue where you left off. Let me know if you need anything, because I am here for you. Please help me get started in seeing the vision as you saw it so many years before. I don't got much money or a car, but I got my bitch and we will do what you need. I am not into fuckin' around. We can help each other. You can write me at: Jason Moss, 1234 My Place, Henderson, NV 89014. I look forward to hearing from you soon. By the way, John says "hi."

Your faithful friend,
Jason Moss

In this letter, I attempted something I'd never tried before—using a fictitious person as an excuse for writing someone a letter. Since most of the people writing to Manson would want something—an interview, a souvenir, or his time—I knew he'd be more likely to respond if he didn't think that I wanted something from him but rather that I was in a position to help him.

I portrayed myself as a poor, angry man—yet also a leader who'd do whatever it took to make things "right" again in society. I wanted him to think I was a good investment of his time, worth spending energy "grooming." Whereas Gacy responded to weakness, Manson, I figured, would be drawn to some degree of strength, especially if it was clear that I'd remain within his control.

On many television interviews I'd heard him state that he wasn't into games, so by stating "I am not into fuckin' around," I hoped that he'd identify with my directness. I didn't worry much about him taking the bait; after all, I already had Gacy to talk to, and I was forming plans to reach out to other killers as well. I knew it was unrealistic to think I could get everyone to write back.

Just a few days later, though, I received a postcard from Manson in which he presented a test of my intentions. Writing in broken, schoolboy English, he stated that he'd give *me* something if I'd give him what *he* wanted. Initially, this was subscriptions to magazines. He admitted he'd never heard of "that person in NY," but it didn't surprise him that much, since he received so much mail. "I learn not to write letters," Manson explained, "because people play and use you for things beyond your wild dreams. They say all they will do and lie—you will see as you get old."

A postcard was the last thing I expected to receive from Manson. My address wasn't even legible on the card and at first I wondered how it could possibly have been delivered. Then it occurred to me that Cynthia, our mail lady, must have been so used to routing me letters from Gacy's prison she figured it had to be for me.

The next day I was able to confirm my suspicion. I was walking out to the mailbox just as Cynthia had finished inserting the last of the letters when I noticed she had a big grin on her face.

"What's so funny?" I asked her a little nervously. She was probably beginning to think I was some kind of weirdo.

"Nothing," she answered a bit hesitantly. I could tell this was awkward for her.

"Go on," I said.

"It's just that . . . I don't know, Jason. Sometimes, when I'm driving on my route and I approach your stop, I can't believe what you're doing. Your mail is just so unusual. You're always getting letters from prisons and stuff. I couldn't help but look at the envelopes. You don't mind, do you?"

I couldn't believe this was happening. The mail lady was actually monitoring my letters. Actually, I was flattered. Cynthia is a nice person.

"So," she asked me, "what the heck does this Gacy guy tell you?"

"Nothin' much," I replied. "I usually ask him things about the prison system and capital punishment."

"God, just yesterday, some of the guys at work were asking what type of person you were."

"Really?" I answered. *Now they're talking about me at the post office!*

"Yeah. I told them you're this really sweet, brilliant future psychologist who just likes to study these people. The whole station talks about you."

"They do?" I said, more than a little embarrassed. "A lot of people think what I'm doing is kind of weird. That's why I pretty much just keep things to myself."

"I understand," she said. "You know, when you got that letter from Manson yesterday, I dropped it on the ground in disbelief. It was so scary to touch something that you know *he* touched. It was so eerie."

"Hey," I said, "thanks for getting it to me. I know how awful his handwriting is."

"No problem. The guys were going to label it undeliverable, but when they said it was on my route, I knew it must be for you."

After that day, I never had a problem getting Manson's letters no matter how unintelligible the address was.

With Gacy, it might have just been blind luck. But now that Manson had written back, I was pretty impressed with myself. I developed what would turn out to be a false confidence regarding my ability to "play" these people—fed, no doubt, by the illiterate way in which they expressed themselves.

Manson's writing, for example, looked like the product of an eight-year-old, and a very demented one at that. Further, he just assumed that others knew what he was talking about when he left stuff out of the middle of his sentences.

In his postcard, he reminded me that he was not into playing games either. I confronted a dilemma: if I refused his request for magazine subscriptions, he might interpret the refusal as a lack of commitment; if, however, I showed immediate subservience, he might write me off as just another fan whom he could dominate. I wanted him to know that I was someone to be reckoned with.

As a compromise, I wrote him back and told him I didn't have much money so I couldn't afford to send him anything. I did say, though, that I hoped my financial situation would improve and that I'd send him a subscription in a month or two.

I'd become accustomed to Gacy's long, rambling, detailed letters, so by contrast, Manson's replies seemed even more stark and enigmatic. His next communication came almost immediately. It was just one line long but included a reading list of authors and books he wanted me to become familiar with. He was going to be my tutor and I his student. He wanted me to start with Kahlil Gibran's *The Prophet* and a few others I'd never heard of.

He also included the name and address of another follower of his who could supply me with more material. Now, *that* got me a little worried. Since I was using my real address (just as I had with Gacy, knowing that a post office box would be immediately suspect), it wouldn't be that difficult for one of Manson's family members on the outside to come by and check me out. It occurred to me that Manson must have lots of crazed followers willing to do his bidding. If he'd been able to get someone to attempt an assassination of the president of the United States, he certainly wouldn't find it much of a challenge to dispatch someone to my house to see if I was all I said I was. My parents were somewhat tolerant, but I figured they'd draw the line if I told them I'd invited a few friends over for dinner—but, not to worry, "we're all part of Charles Manson's family."

In what was in retrospect one of my more ill-considered acts, I actually contacted the individual Manson had referred me to, and the disciple supplied me with an array of reading materials, religious books, Manson videos, and others to contact in my own area who had similar views. The mailings had a comic aspect. I half expected to be recruited for a "get out the vote for Manson" drive come the next election.

The disciple told me he was really busy, so I only received three packages from him. Last Christmas, though, he sent me a letter telling me he'd moved, and he was there if I needed him. I passed along all of this information to the local office of the FBI, although I have no idea what they did with it.

20

Deeply Disturbed

Once Manson started to trust me, he began lecturing and teaching me about dozens of different topics that seemed randomly chosen. Sometimes, for no apparent reason, he'd become enraged; at other times he'd be very gentle and sensitive. I never knew what to expect.

I repeatedly tried to reassure him that I was safe, that I could be trusted with his innermost thoughts and feelings. To him, though, the very fact that I'd brought up trust as an issue meant I planned to be deceitful toward him. I was also giving him the runaround regarding those magazines he wanted.

After corresponding with Manson for only a short time, however, my interest in him diminished. He was not a "real" serial killer to me, but more of a cult leader who got others to do his killing for him. Further, I'd come to realize that he wasn't ever going to be able to communicate on the level I desired, and the constant rambling in his letters began to grow tiresome and confusing. He was also very paranoid, often accusing me of betraying him. In one letter, he became very irate and frustrated because I hadn't yet sent him some stuff he'd ordered.

"First I got no books," Manson complained, "and its clear by your words that you were razed & taught how to bullshit your own thoughts & pay rent to live in your old life. Your a gamer & start out hiding behind your own words about what you think is all yourself."

Of course, he had reason to be paranoid. I *was* being deceitful and dishonest with him. It was sensible of him to mistrust my motives.

In particular, it really seemed to bother him that I was a student, because that meant I aspired to be part of the establishment. He raged on and on, incoherently screaming at me in his letters that I wasn't worthy of his trust. "I know a hole system of people like you," he wrote, "who hide in books & schools & live on paper computing banks & past. I already got some books thanks—How long you been working in the mail room unless you make the rules in the mail room."

In referring to me as working in the mail room, he was voicing his suspicion that I was working him "from the inside," meaning within the prison itself. It might seem as if he'd caught on to me, but that wasn't the case at all. He was merely testing me. If he truly believed what he said, then he wouldn't have written back at all. Some weeks, he received over ten pounds of mail. Consequently, he was very selective in his replies.

I hoped that by being aggressive toward him, by letting him know that I wasn't in awe of his notoriety, I'd prompt him to reevaluate me. And sure enough, when I began pushing him more instead of acting apologetic, he responded more authentically, even sending me poems that, while I couldn't exactly understand them, did have a certain eerie power. Written on his personal stationery, with a watermark of his eyes staring at me in the background, the lines of gibberish ran down the page: "Be Bop, Boot & Shoe ding dong the bell has been rang."

The combination of his words and those eyes looking at me disturbed me greatly. Even though it was impossible to impose any meaning on the gibberish, it still felt like *something* was coming across. In occasional moments of self-awareness, I realized I was becoming polluted by Manson's evil, crazy thoughts.

Therapists have reported that when they allow themselves to get close to very disturbed people, they sometimes experience some of their despair, hopelessness, and destructive urges. This applied to me, because after I read some of Manson's letters, even more so than after reading Gacy's, I felt like I needed to take a shower to cleanse myself of the weirdness.

I wondered if Manson was consciously aware of all the things he did to manipulate and control others. So in one of my letters I decided to get the answer to this question indirectly by asking him how I should spread his word to others.

As usual, I didn't understand his response. He seemed to be telling me that you can't really teach anyone anything: "They TEACH you one world but when you go to LIVE what you forget you learn that people has been BULL shiting you—you cant find your self in any one else—you are your own experiences & they cant teach you your life."

It was frustrating to deal with a person who communicated so strangely, even in response to direct questions. I tend to be hyperlogical, so Manson was an especially difficult challenge for me. I kept asking him about how I could survive in the world, how I should follow his teachings, how I could bring others under my/his control, and his responses were all over the map. He seemed to have the attention span of a gnat.

He kept sending me songs, poems, lectures, and scraps of his philosophy, even if I could understand very little of what he was driving at. Perhaps a trained forensic psychologist could venture some informed guesses about what Manson was referring to, or what he was trying to say, but, to me, most of it was the ramblings of a lost soul.

In writing back to him, I acted on the assumption that he made sense to himself at least. Accordingly, I tried to quote some of his more intelligible sayings so he'd know I was listening to him and that we used the same language. I hoped he'd think that I understood how he felt. For the most part, though, I was operating in the dark.

There was one aspect to our correspondence that I found particularly intriguing: almost all of his letters were written on the back of others that had been sent to him. At first, I wondered if he was short of paper but then I learned that he had his own special stationery. It seemed like he was mocking those who'd written to him, and sharing his disdain with me. For example, on the back of one note he sent was the following letter that was fairly typical of those he received:

Dear Mr. Manson,

I am a criminal psychology major at CSU, Long Beach and I am currently working on my thesis paper. I was wondering if I could ask you a big favor. I thought it would be good to

include a section on the current Judicial System and its laws. Do you think you could write
a short commentary on this subject for me to
include as an example I could cite from? It
would mean a lot to me and I would really appreciate it.

The naiveté of this approach surprised me. Couldn't this
student see that he was presenting himself as the figure
Manson hated the most, the elite "man" who was responsible for putting society in the position it was in? It was no
surprise that Manson ran his illegible script over the back of
the young man's words.

In one instance, Manson actually referred directly to one
of the letters written on the back. The letter read as follows:

Dear Mr. Manson,

After two years in prison, I know you have
been contacted by every person under the sun.
I am writing due to the fact I collect notorious people's signatures. I have read your
book several times and feel your signature
would be one of the best in the collection. I
have no opinion on why you are in prison, but
because you are there is the only reason I'm
writing. So Sir, if you want to write back it
would be great. If not I understand but either
way I just want your signature. Thank you.

It astounded me that someone would believe any incarcerated person, let alone the sought-after Charles Manson,

would respond to such a request. You'd think people would do a minimum of research to increase the odds of a response.

Apparently, Manson agreed. "It's hard for me to understand how smart people can be so dum," he wrote on this note, "none of them books have been by or for me—you think there is law & maybe for the rich there is. But when your unschooled people do what makes money. That book is total and complete BUNKUM I never gave no one permission for any books."

This statement showed another side of Manson. It demonstrated that he felt manipulated, that he experienced emotional pain. I found it interesting that he was willing to share these feelings of hurt and betrayal with me in a way that Gacy would never do. Although I never forgot for a moment what a frightening monster Manson was, at times he seemed awfully pathetic and vulnerable.

In my next letter to him, I asked if he encountered any demons or monsters after he fell asleep. I didn't really know where I was going with this, but it seemed like an interesting area to explore. "Here is a card of a monster," Manson replied, "so bad it will eat the hearts of all who put themselves between me & my lone soul self world."

I interpreted Manson's comment about being a "lone soul" as a reference to his earlier days when he believed he was the son of God. He set himself apart from others by creating a mission for himself. In prison this belief only seemed to be reinforced by all the people writing him for guidance.

Once I'd concluded I'd learned all I could about Manson from his letters, I began contemplating visiting him in prison. I planned to drive to the California State Prison during my summer vacation. That would give me enough time, I figured, to gradually let him know how young I was.

Although my assumption was that a visit to Gacy would be low-risk, I expected Manson to be wild, spontaneous—even terrifying. In video footage I'd watched of him, I'd seen him jumping on tables or throwing things at people. Although I suspected he behaved that way partly to enhance his mystique, there was no guarantee he wouldn't behave the same way with me.

With all the research I was doing, and all the success I was encountering, my hopes increased that someday the FBI might want to hire me as a psychologist and serial killer profiler. What had begun as a whim—writing letters to the people I'd read about in my true-crime books—had evolved into a methodology for winning the trust of some of the most murderous human beings ever. And the risks involved were slight—or so I believed.

After striking pay dirt with Gacy and Manson, I couldn't help wondering whom else I could get to.

21

Cannibal

A thousand dollars for just one of Charles Manson's signatures? You've got to be kidding!"

I was flabbergasted. I couldn't believe that anyone would pay that kind of money for a mere envelope Manson had once addressed.

"Yeah," the owner of the autograph store said, sneering. "So what's it to you?"

I didn't like this guy. He was a small man, but cocky for someone who looked so young and frail. He had a wispy mustache that made him seem even younger than his thirty-odd years. He'd started out with a small personal collection of autographs and somehow built it into a business. Now he owned stores all over the country.

I didn't ordinarily frequent such establishments, especially in this upscale area of Vegas that catered largely to wealthy tourists who had extra time and money on their hands. While their husbands played blackjack or craps at the neighboring casinos, the wives could be seen roaming the high-priced boutiques with a frantic determination to spend their own share of the family income.

The small autograph store specialized in celebrity arti-facts. In the window was a guitar once played by Jimi Hen-drix, a baseball bat signed by Joe DiMaggio, and an assortment of documents bearing the signatures of famous politicians, athletes, and movie stars. I'd heard that the col-lection included some serial killer autographs as well, which is why I'd made a point of stopping by.

"Excuse me, sir," I'd begun with as much restraint as I could muster, "but I was just wondering what the market is like for letters and stuff from famous killers."

The owner sighed. But it was a slow day. And I was his only customer. "It all depends on what you've got."

I nodded. I was the eager student, attentive and polite.

"You see," he explained, "you've got your basic killers. They're not worth much because there's so much of their stuff around." Almost in spite of himself, he seemed to warm to the subject.

"What about Gacy?" I interrupted.

"He's about average, I'd say. He's pretty famous but he writes a lot of people."

"What if I had several dozen letters?" I asked. "All of them are very explicit in describing his sexual tastes, his life in prison, his feelings about his crimes."

The man cocked his head to the side, looking at me seri-ously for the first time. "Are you yanking my chain or something?"

"No," I said agreeably. "I was just wondering what the letters were worth. I'm not interested in selling them."

I could see the owner's expression change, greed now replacing skepticism. "C'mon," he whined, "you'll sell eventually. Everyone's got their price."

It was sort of fun watching him wheedle. "I was just

wondering who's worth the most. I mean, which serial killer's autograph is the most valuable?"

He thought for just a moment before he replied. "That would be Jeffrey Dahmer, the cannibal guy who ate his victims."

"Yeah?" I said. "What's so special about him?"

The owner looked at me condescendingly. "Dahmer just doesn't like to write people. His stuff is extremely rare. I think there's only one guy in the whole country who has any letters from him."

"Is that right?" I said, my mind working. I was pretty sure whom I'd be contacting next.

As I walked out of the store my head was spinning with possibilities. First, I couldn't believe how valuable my collection of letters was—dealers like the one I'd just spoken to would pay me five thousand dollars for the Gacy material, and even more for my letters from Manson. I hadn't contacted these killers for the potential profit involved, and wouldn't start now. Still, to a penniless college student, these sums were pretty dazzling.

I tried to recall what I knew about Jeffrey Dahmer. Not much, really. I remembered that he not only captured, tortured, and killed young boys but also *ate* them. I thought it interesting that he hadn't written to anyone. Might it be that the grisliness of his crimes had put off even those who tend to glom on to celebrity killers? Or perhaps he'd vowed not to communicate with the outside world, had quite literally written it off.

It was time to do some research. I began by calling the Milwaukee Police Department and ordering a copy of Dahmer's 230-page confession. This would give me a starting point, a feel for the way he thought and talked.

When the thick package from Wisconsin arrived, I was so overwhelmed with schoolwork that I had no time to examine the contents until the following day. I decided to find a quiet spot in the Student Union Building to sit and peruse the transcript for a few minutes before class.

As I approached the entrance, I noticed the familiar sights that make campus life so interesting and fun. Kids throwing Frisbees on the new-mown lawn. Skateboarders and rollerbladers gliding past, using pedestrians as their moving slalom course. Dedicated students studying in pairs or alone under the shade of trees. I don't think I'd have been incorrect to assume that at that moment no one—other than me—was brooding about man-eating serial killers.

After finding a vacant table inside, I became so engrossed in the dialogue that had taken place between Jeffrey Dahmer and a homicide detective that I lost all track of time and place. Despite the dry police verbiage, I was glued to the page. Automatically, I kept translating the dry, clinical legalese into the conversation I imagined took place between this cannibal who was more than willing to talk about his craft, and the experienced detective who acted like he'd heard it all before.

"So, Mr. Dahmer," the detective asked politely, "how did you go about disposing of your victims?"

"Well," Dahmer replied just as matter-of-factly, "I'd just drag the body into the bathtub."

Dahmer hesitated for a moment, lost in thought, as if he was reliving the experience all over again.

"Go on," the detective prodded gently. "Then what happened?"

Dahmer shrugged. "First, I'd strip off all the clothes on

My younger brother, Jarrod (*left*), me, and our dog, Smokey.

Cynthia, the mail carrier on my route, worried about the letters from
John Wayne Gacy and Charles Manson.

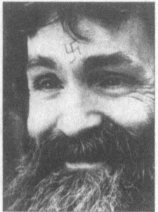

Shortly before his murder in prison, I corresponded with Jeffrey Dahmer, who was both shy and sexually graphic in his letters. (*Reuters/Corbis-Bettman*)

My request to join Manson's "family" was answered by manic ravings and a list of "required reading." (*UPI/Corbis-Bettman*)

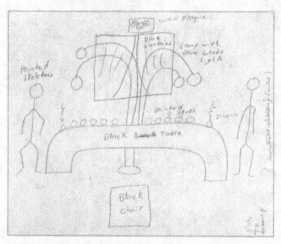

Jeffrey Dahmer's sketched plans to construct a temple out of body parts. (*AP/Wide World Photos*)

Henry Lee Lucas (*left*), pictured here after having led police to the scene of a double homicide in California, related his tips for killing when I visited him in prison. (*AP/Wide World Photos*)

Lucas, who is reputed to have killed as many as 100 people, sent me this oddly serene watercolor of a lighthouse. (*Henry Lee Lucas/ Photographed by Kelly Garni*)

"Night Stalker" Richard Ramirez responded enthusiastically to my letters, boasting of murdering and raping his victims as a tribute to Satan. (*AP/Wide World Photos*)

Every letter Ramirez sent me was decorated with pentagrams, the symbol for Satanism. (*AP/Wide World Photos*)

Richard Ramirez always included drawings with his correspondence. (*Richard Ramirez/ Photographed by Kelly Garni*)

"Monster." (*Richard Ramirez/Photographed by Kelly Garni*)

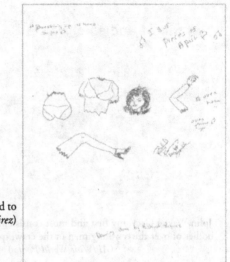

"Breaking Up Is Hard to Do." (*Richard Ramirez*)

"Trophy Collection." (*Richard Ramirez*)

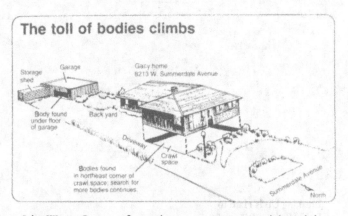

The toll of bodies climbs

Storage shed

Garage

Gacy home
8213 W. Summerdale Avenue

Body found
under floor
of garage

Back yard

Driveway

Crawl
space

Bodies found
in northeast corner of
crawl space; search for
more bodies continues.

Summerdale Avenue

North

John Wayne Gacy, my first and most consistent pen pal, buried the
bodies of over thirty young men in the crawl space under his house.
(*AP/Wide World Photos*)

John Wayne Gacy's
mug shot, taken twenty
years ago. (*AP/Wide
World Photos*)

John Wayne Gacy's last home, the Menard Correctional Center in Chester, Illinois.

Caught in a twisted web of my own making, I visited John Wayne Gacy in his Illinois prison, where he showed his true colors at last.

Murderer of eight women and a friend of Gacy's on Death Row, Andrew "Koko" Kokoralies looked intimidating but trusted me almost immediately.

My experience with the serial killers and my desire to become an FBI profiler led to an internship with the Secret Service, during which I met President and Mrs. Bush.

the body. Then, I took off my clothes too so they wouldn't get dirty. I'd get in the tub too."

The detective nodded his head, indicating that he was listening intently.

"I'd use a sharp knife," Dahmer continued, "a very sharp knife. For something like this, it has to be very sharp."

Again the detective nodded, as if he understood perfectly the problems of cutting up bodies with something less than suitable instruments.

"I'd start at the top of the chest and cut all the way down. Then I'd spread it open and remove all the—"

"Wait a minute," the detective interrupted. "Slow down. What do you mean you'd spread—"

"You know, I'd peel the skin and muscle back. That way I could scoop out all the stuff inside."

The detective nodded, drinking from his cold coffee to take the sour taste from his mouth. Dahmer just looked dreamy-eyed, sitting there talking about butchering a body as easily as preparing a chicken for the barbecue.

"I'd cut up all the organs and put them into plastic bags. Each piece would be about the size of my fist." He held out his hand to show the detective what he meant.

I was hanging on to every word of this narration when someone called out to me. "Jason! Hey, Jason!"

"Hey, guy," I responded groggily. It was like I'd been on a different planet. I couldn't remember his name but I recognized him from one of my classes.

"Aren't you supposed to be in class now?" he asked.

"Oh, shit!"

I'd been so immersed in the transcript that I'd completely forgotten where I was. A whole hour had gone by just like that, and I was still less than halfway through.

"Screw it," I thought, and maybe even said it aloud to my classmate. I was already late for class, so I figured I might as well finish what I'd started. Besides, I reasoned, this was a hell of a lot more interesting than some boring lecture.

I settled back into my seat, propped my feet up on the chair next to me, and returned to one of the most bizarre conversations I'd ever read.

"Okay," the detective summarized. "So you were saying that it took about five bags for each body. Tell me, what were you feeling or thinking about during all this? I mean, you know—"

"Um. It's all kind of exciting." Dahmer thought for a moment, then continued, "But I was also scared. I didn't want to get caught and this was the most dangerous time."

"Yes," the detective agreed, encouraging him to continue.

"I also felt this intense loss as I threw the bags into the garbage. At one time, these bags of body parts were a human being with a whole life in front of him. Now they were nothing but garbage. A complete waste."

"So you did feel kind of bad about it afterwards?" the detective said, leading him to a place that felt familiar.

"Yeah. Sure I did." Dahmer nodded to himself as much as to the detective. "It just didn't seem like I could help myself. It's all I could do."

Wow! This was amazing stuff, I thought. Not only was Dahmer willing to admit to his crimes, but he talked freely about what drove him to kill. He struck me as very transparent, almost meek—not at all like Gacy or Manson, who could be so aggressive. If only I could get accustomed to the revolting details of Dahmer's crimes, it seemed like this challenge would be far easier than I imagined.

22

Only the Lonely

I walked out of the Student Union that afternoon almost certain I could find some way to capture Dahmer's interest. And over the next few weeks I read every book and article I could find on him. When that still didn't seem enough, I watched every piece of news footage I could locate. I also read about other killers throughout history who'd operated in similar ways.

Dahmer's childhood seemed especially intriguing. From all accounts, he'd grown up very alone, with no one to really share things with. Much of his behavior seemed calculated to achieve companionship without risk of hurt or rejection.

As I reviewed his history further, I learned that he'd been charged with the murder of fifteen males—all homosexual, all young, mostly minorities. When he was arrested, the remains of eleven victims were found in acid vats in his apartment, as well as in his refrigerator. So fond was he of keeping mementos of his victims that he would typically sever their heads, boil them in water, and save the skulls—either in a box or in a discreet place in his bedroom.

At the time of his arrest, there was a human head found in his refrigerator, as well as a human heart and a biceps, which he planned on eating later. It was his habit to eat a portion of each victim, particularly those he especially liked, because this allowed him to keep a part of them inside him.

His usual killing strategy was to lure a young man to his apartment for an evening of entertainment. While fixing his guest a drink, he'd add sleeping pills to knock him out. After the guest was unconscious, Dahmer would strangle him. Sometimes he had sex with his victims when they were alive, but he'd usually have oral and anal sex with the corpse.

As if this wasn't sick enough, he sometimes kept the dead bodies around long enough to watch maggots crawling in and out of the rotting flesh. Even at that level of extreme decomposition, he'd still find the bodies appealing enough to have sex with them.

On a scale of revulsion, this was indisputably at the top of anyone's list. Gacy, or even Manson, seemed downright civilized by comparison. This was one reason that the idea of getting to Dahmer appealed to me—he just seemed so incomprehensible, so *alien*. I could understand why people might kill others, why they might rape, or even why they might torture victims to express rage. But Dahmer—he was a new *species* of deviant.

Imagine coming home from work each day to a house littered with body parts from people you've murdered and mutilated. Given his demonic behavior, it was particularly ironic that Dahmer looked so frail and ordinary. To anyone who contemplated this man and his acts long enough, much of the terror he evoked was attributable to there being little about him that might warn anyone what he was capable of.

The experts agreed that Dahmer's most prominent traits were (1) a powerful sexual appetite and (2) a pathological fear of being alone. In looking for an angle to attract Dahmer's attention, I knew I had to operate quite differently than I had with Gacy, for example. Dahmer was only interested in physical control; he displayed no interest in psychological games. Gacy needed his victims alive when he played with them, but Dahmer didn't. He was just trying to keep "the boys" with him at all times. He had no interest in proving his power or superiority; he just didn't want to be alone.

Ultimately, I decided that Dahmer should see me as a boy all alone in a world just as depraved as his. Pain, misery, sexual confusion—I'd show him all these traits, hoping he'd recognize himself in my story. My goal was to get him to share some coping advice drawn from his own experiences, or better yet, ways he tried to avoid the pain. My introductory letter to him reads as follows:

Dear Jeff,

My name is Jason Moss, and I'm writing you this letter because it's very late at night where I am, and I'm taking care of my sick grandmother. She's been throwing up all night and I'm afraid she's going to die. If she dies, I'll be all alone.

Both of my parents were killed in a car crash last year, and I now have to live with my grandmother. I feel very alone and scared,

and sometimes I just want to die. I feel like
I live in a world all alone, far from everyone. I've heard about the things they say
you've done, and I understand how you feel not
wanting to be alone, and all. I feel like I
need a strong man in my life, and sometimes I
just think about holding one of my friends,
giving him a hug, and never letting go. Maybe
we can be friends. Is there anything you need
there in prison? Is there anything I can do
for you like sending some magazines? My address is: Jason Moss, 1234 My Place, Henderson, NV 89014. I'd really appreciate hearing
from you. Knowing that there is someone out
there who cares might make living a little
easier. Have a happy new year.

Your friend,
Jason Moss

I thought my story would sound very familiar to Dahmer.
Just as he had felt when growing up, I appeared to be very
alone, depressed, and scared. I hoped that by making him
think my parents were both killed in a car crash, he'd believe there was a possibility I could empathize with his own
loneliness.

Writing him my first letter, I couldn't help feeling there
was some truth to the things I told him. At times, I *did* feel
like I was all alone in the world. Even though I had a family that was mostly supportive, a girlfriend I was fond of,
and a number of friends I'd known since junior high school,
I still felt different and alienated sometimes. Of course, this

was because I *was* different. Neither my friends nor my family could relate to my ambition—or my capacity for tunnel vision. There were very few people, including Jenn, who really understood me. Hence, it wasn't that difficult to write even a fictitious letter like this with some conviction.

In spite of the elation I was feeling over the solid preparation that went into writing Dahmer, there was a spillover that was taking its toll on me emotionally. Though I didn't fully realize it at the time, obsessively reading about necrophilia and cannibalism was beyond the limits of what I could handle. It can't be very good for even a trained psychologist or detective to think about murder all the time, to empathize both with the perpetrators of the most horrible crimes ever committed and with their victims. Just imagine what such reflection can do to a first-year college student whose experience of the world has been confined to one metropolitan area.

My obsession was isolating me further. More and more often, I began avoiding my friends. Jenn and I broke up for a while, not just because of my latest project but because of conflicts over diverging life goals. There was also continual tension at home, including fights between—and with—my parents, and even some distancing on Jarrod's part.

To my deepening dismay, I was becoming like the monsters I was studying—not in their homicidal urges, but in their perceived separation from the rest of society. I only learned later—when I took developmental psychology classes—how normal these feelings are for someone of my age, but at the time I just accepted that I was weird. This belief was continuously reinforced by my parents and peers, who were constantly teasing me because of my strange interests.

If I had stopped to think about it at the time (which I certainly didn't, or I would never have continued my morbid project), I would have realized that the people with whom I had the most intimate relationships were all imprisoned serial killers. Even worse than that, these supposed friendships were built on lies and deception.

From everything I later read in my developmental psychology textbooks, my primary job at this stage was to develop close affiliations with people my age. This was becoming increasingly difficult as I retreated deeper and deeper into myself, unwilling to trust anyone with what I was doing. In a way, my reticence was a good thing—or I wouldn't have had any friends at all!

During this period in which I was maintaining correspondence with Gacy, Manson, and now Dahmer, I was losing the part of myself that was most familiar. My thoughts previously centered around doing well in school, preparing myself for a good career, learning things in my classes, going out with friends, and spending time with my girlfriend. Now I was constantly thinking about the various murderers I was studying. Even more disturbing, I was beginning to identify with them. I felt sorry for them. I shared their pain. I understood their motivations. I was even making excuses for them: they couldn't help the way they were. It wasn't their choice; they were made that way.

I began to see darkness in everyone I came in contact with, and pitied every naive potential victim I'd see as well. I lost all of my faith in God. I began to see the world as a place consisting of the weak and the strong. The hunters and the hunted.

For several months, I read almost nothing else except story after story, article after article, about death. Looking back, I see now that I should have forced myself to take a break. Even some FBI investigators have to rotate their job duties every once in a while to prevent severe psychological damage. Clearly, I was walking a mental tightrope.

Of course if a teacher, therapist, or even a concerned adult had been monitoring what I was doing, they might have helped me gain some perspective on what was happening to me. The only person in my life who was really acting like much of a mentor, though, was John Wayne Gacy.

No wonder I was in trouble.

23

Doubts

After I sent the letter off to Dahmer, I waited impatiently for a reply. I'd been spoiled by Gacy's and Manson's timely responses, so I became more and more anxious as the days flew by without any answer. I second-guessed myself continuously. Had I made the right decision to hold back a photograph of me? I wanted Dahmer to write back and ask for something. Perhaps I hadn't given him enough to pique his curiosity. Maybe I should have tried a different strategy altogether.

Weeks passed without a reply. In frustration, I redoubled my attention toward Gacy and Manson. I also made plans to contact other serial killers like Richard "the Night Stalker" Ramirez and Henry Lee Lucas. I even began questioning everything I'd done so far. Maybe I'd just been extremely fortunate up to this point. Maybe I was just some weirdo kid who'd lucked onto a couple psycho pen pals.

I tried to console myself as best I could. The autograph dealer *did* say that nobody ever got letters from Dahmer, so it was probably unrealistic to think I could pull this off. At least Dahmer's reluctance to reply had made my mother happy.

"You see, Jason," she rubbed it in one day, "you can't get letters from all of these guys. Why don't you just let it go and concentrate on school?"

I wished she hadn't looked so pleased by my failure; that only encouraged me to prove she was wrong. "Aw, Mom, please don't start with me."

As it turned out, my mother had rejoiced too soon. At the end of January, just when I'd given up on Dahmer altogether, there was a letter from him in the mail. I was so happy that I couldn't keep from screaming right in front of my own mailbox. My very first thought was to run in immediately and show my mother she'd been wrong.

"Mom, look at this baby!" I yelled as I ran into the kitchen, where she was preparing dinner. I could see her eyes roll. "Dahmer finally did write me back. God, I can't believe I ever doubted myself."

My mother put down the knife she was using to chop vegetables. She gave me that stern look, the one that said she really means what she's about to say. Now it was my turn to roll my eyes.

"Jason," she declared, "you've taken this too far. This has *got* to stop."

At bottom, I realized this argument wasn't really about Dahmer's letter, or even about my serial killer project. Ever since I could remember, my mother and I played out this little war in which she'd tell me I couldn't do something and then I'd set out to prove her wrong. We were both pretty stubborn, so things would usually end in a truce that allowed us both to save face. This time, though, I was going to rub it in all I could.

"See, Mom," I bored in, "I *told* you I could do this. Why can't you ever feel proud of the things I do?"

"But I *am* proud of you, honey. It's just—"

That's about as far as the conversation got before I made a hasty retreat, or rather a strategic withdrawal. I knew where this was headed and I didn't want to go there. I was in too good a mood right then to fight with her.

I ran up to my room, locked the door, and ripped open the envelope to find a two-page letter written by a man who seemed very gracious, even scrupulously polite. Dahmer thanked me for writing, wished me a happy new year, and then apologized profusely for taking so long to respond. "I'm a much better talker than writer," he said, "so I don't always keep up with the mail as I should."

He then went on to mention that he was indeed interested in having me arrange for some magazine subscriptions. He named several titles that I later learned were explicit gay publications. Apparently, prisoners weren't allowed to order their own magazines or newspapers; they had to be sent as gifts.

Finally, he asked that I send him a photo of myself, anything other than a Polaroid for some reason. Then he signed off by saying he hoped to hear from me again real soon.

That this letter meant the world to me was an indication of how far gone I was. Everything I'd predicted Dahmer would do came true. He'd even asked for a photo. Now I agonized over whether to send him some subscriptions or make him wait longer.

In my response to him, I included the safest photo I could find. I wasn't all that comfortable thinking about

Dahmer gazing at my picture for hours. Would he be selecting the piece of me he wanted to eat?

I spent the better part of that evening locked in my room, thinking about how to construct my response to him. When I heard my parents come upstairs, I snuck into the kitchen to load up on food for what I knew would be another sleepless night.

In the brief reply I wrote to Dahmer, I said that although I was a struggling college student I'd ordered the magazines he requested. I deliberately kept my letter brief so that my photo would have more impact. I believed it was the visual image of another potential victim that would most appeal to him.

This time, I didn't have to wait long to hear back. He must have written me immediately after he read my letter. His response was again extremely polite, although accompanying the gracious words was a provocative photo of a naked man with a full erection. It obviously set the tone for the content of the words to come and represented a rather obvious attempt to seduce me.

He had much to say about the photo I'd sent him:

> It looks like you have a great "swimmer's" build, although it's a bit hard to tell because you're bent over in the picture. You certainly do have a handsome face. I'm glad you didn't send a "polaroid," because they don't allow us to keep them. They're afraid someone will lick the chemicals off the bottom strip or something.

He went on to give me detailed instructions regarding the additional photos he wanted me to send:

> I'd like to see full body shots of you lying on the bed, hands behind your head, with your chest fully inflated. I'd enjoy photos of you reaching high for the ceiling. To me, there's nothing more erotic than a handsome young man with a rock hard body and a slim tapering waist.

I couldn't decide if I should feel flattered or utterly repulsed that he found me attractive. I suppose a little of both. I *was* pleased that he'd decided to trust me. He confided that the reason he didn't normally respond to letters is that people always wanted something from him, usually his autograph. Apparently, he'd been disappointed previously in regard to things others had promised that they hadn't delivered.

The letter ended with another apology for his photo requests: "Sorry, I don't mean to sound demanding, it's just that you've caught my interest; which is not always an easy thing to do!"

I anticipated that Dahmer would display mild intelligence and very average social abilities. I knew that the way he gained control over his victims was by drugging them. This was not the act of someone who was very confident or sophisticated in his interpersonal skills.

I hoped that as soon as I earned more of his trust, he'd be willing to really open up to me, as well as possibly let me visit him. I could already see early signs that he was relating to me just as he did to his prospective victims. He'd typically lure boys into his apartment by offering them money to pose for him. Once they were in his lair, he'd make sure they never left.

At the end of Dahmer's letter he wrote, "I'll be happy to accommodate you in the future *if* you'll accommodate me."

Quite frankly, this made me nervous. Gacy and Manson hadn't been as direct in their requests as Dahmer. I was concerned he was getting too close, too fast. It reminded me of the saying "Be careful of what you wish for because you just might get it."

In spite of my ambivalence, I sent Dahmer another letter in which I enclosed a picture of me at the beach with my shirt off, playing with some friends. I hoped that would hold him for a while, so I could get back to other aspects of my project—Gacy, Manson, et al.—that needed attention. I also told him I had some major exams to prepare for, so I'd write him again in a couple of weeks.

He responded immediately:

```
     ...your school work is important, and I
completely understand your needing time for
finals. Just don't forget about me when your
school work is done, ha ha. I have many things
to do to keep myself busy anyway. Let me know
when you're ready to pursue a serious rela-
tionship. As long as you have the time with-
out distraction, I would be more than open to
it.
```

Of course, neither of us realized that Dahmer had a date with destiny—shortly after, he was murdered in prison by another inmate. Ironically, while most of the country was celebrating his death—or at least saying "good riddance"— I was feeling upset and disappointed. Here I had this great opportunity to explore Dahmer's mind and learn things about the way he thought and operated, and, in an instant, that opportunity was snuffed out.

21

Night Stalker

What are you doing *now*, Jason?" my father said with exasperation. He was on his way to bed and noticed my light was still on. When he peered into my room, it looked like a strong wind had blown papers all over the place. I was sitting on the floor in the middle of the mess, putting the papers into an orderly sequence.

"Nothing much," I said, hoping he'd go off to bed. I didn't want to lose my concentration.

"Looks like homework or something," he observed.

"Yeah," I said noncommittally without looking up.

"Well, okay, I'm off to bed."

"Night, Dad."

Once I could hear his footsteps padding off, I sighed, both in relief and in disappointment. I really did want to tell him what I was doing, but I also realized it could mean trouble. I was in no mood for another lecture.

What I'd been involved with when my father interrupted was trying to bring some organization to all the correspondence I'd been receiving lately. Although, in re-creating what occurred, I've given the impression that my approaches to Gacy, Manson, and Dahmer were sequential, there was actually a good deal of overlap. Even after I spread out all the letters on the floor of my room, ordering them chronologically, I still felt unsure of the timeline. Truthfully, this two-month period in my life from December to February of my freshman year had become very confusing.

About the same time I first wrote Dahmer, I also sent a letter to Richard Ramirez, called the Night Stalker because of his modus operandi in terrorizing Southern California during 1984–85. During his rampage, Ramirez broke into homes indiscriminately, raping women, torturing them, and leaving them for dead. By the time he'd been captured, he'd killed at least fourteen and raped dozens more.

He was far more erratic than most serial killers, who follow some sort of a predictable pattern. In his case, nobody was safe, since he'd randomly select a home, break in, and kill everyone inside. There was almost nothing people could do to prevent themselves from becoming a victim, no matter what their ages. Sometimes Ramirez would snatch young children, rape them, then leave their bodies in random locations throughout the state. In one case, he raped and killed a woman in her mid-eighties. Many of the bodies were found with satanic symbols carved into their flesh. During his trial, Ramirez would smile and wave to cameras, displaying on his hand a satanic pentagram he'd drawn.

As I sat on the floor of my room, reviewing the letters and thinking about whom to write to next, I tried to imagine sleeping in my house, having a wife and family of my own. One night as I lie in bed, a man breaks into the house, shoots me in the chest, and as my life slowly drifts away, he brutally rapes and beats my wife. I can hear the woman I love scream for me to help. I watch as her hands reach out in anguish. As I gasp for breath, I watch him leave my wife, barely alive on the floor, to enter the rooms of my son and daughter . . .

As the fantasy played itself out, it seemed so real that I actually made a point of standing up in my room and looking around to reassure myself that none of this had happened. I'd been reading so much about Ramirez lately that it felt like he was stalking me. I turned on more lights in the room to take away the shadows. I knew another night would pass without my getting much sleep.

Ramirez struck me as very different from any other serial killer I'd yet studied. Rather than lure victims into his own domain, he preferred to enter their worlds and destroy them. Further, he didn't seem to care much about who his prey was.

I also found it interesting that he became sexually aroused during his killing. Police discovered semen not only inside some of the women he raped but also on their torsos. Apparently, Ramirez became so excited as he slashed someone's throat that he'd actually have an orgasm.

There were also significant elements of rage in his behavior. He seemed to thrive on other people's fear—the more, the better. In addition, Satan worship seemed to dominate his thinking. I didn't know much about that stuff, but I intended to bone up on it so I could devise the best approach.

In writing to him, I thought I'd portray myself as the high priest of a satanic cult that was active in Las Vegas. That way, he might see me as a colleague who shared his life's work, similar to the impression I'd tried to create with Manson.

I began my research at the local New Age bookstore, where I found information on black magic, witchcraft, and satanism. For a period of weeks, I devoted myself completely to studying the beliefs, behaviors, and language used by various cults. I learned what various satanic symbols meant so I could include them in the letters I wrote to Ramirez.

Since the bookstore was on the opposite side of town, every time I made the journey it felt like I was traveling to another world. Of course, the very act of crossing the Las Vegas Strip to get to the West Side puts you in the mood for entering other dimensions. I couldn't help but smile as I sat at the light on Flamingo and Las Vegas Boulevard and surveyed six different casinos, each offering visitors another world—from ancient Rome to contemporary Sodom and Gomorrah. Significantly, each of these resort themes seemed tame in comparison to the cult world I was exploring.

The New Age bookstore was very dark inside, kind of spooky actually. There was the scent of incense in the air. I could hear the soothing sounds of harp music in the background, but also the louder melody of falling water. A waterfall had been specially constructed to provide browsers with the atmosphere of a rain forest. Only in Las Vegas.

Every wall was covered with books, charms, talismans, strange religious symbols, viny plants, and spiritual pictures. On the counter there was actually a black cat sleeping. All that was missing was ghostly wailing coming up through the floorboards.

The shopkeeper was an old man, muttering to himself as

he replenished the inventory in glass display cases. There were charms, pentagrams, strange potions, stones, crystals, even daggers. He was so intent on arranging the paraphernalia that he didn't seem to notice me. All I could see in the dim light was the top of his bald head where he'd artfully combed his few wispy hairs, and numerous charms dangling from his neck.

I was examining advertisements for tarot card readings when I heard a raspy voice say, "If I can help you with anything, just let me know." He then continued unloading a box of small bottles.

"Do you have any books on black magic?" I asked.

Without answering, he carefully arranged the position of a bottle and then directed me to follow him to the opposite corner of the store. Again without saying a word, he pointed to a huge selection of books on witchcraft, then started back toward the vicinity of the waterfall.

"Excuse me, sir," I said, stopping him in midshuffle. "Do any of these books talk about satanism or human sacrifices?"

The old man looked at me sternly. "I am a witch. We practice white magic here. I don't know much about black magic, and I recommend you stay away from it yourself." With that pronouncement, he turned away, shaking his head. I was fascinated by the way the sound of his retreating footsteps was swallowed by the water sounds.

I selected several books that seemed relevant to my task, including one called *The Satanic Bible*. As I paid for them at the counter, staring at the twitching tail of the cat as it slept, I could see the man's look of disapproval. I half wondered whether he'd try to cast some sort of spell on me to frustrate my intentions. Thinking on it, I decided it was probably a good thing that at least some of these people had ethical standards.

Since material on satanism and human sacrifice that can be construed as "how to" is usually illegal—and rightfully so!—I was skeptical that these books would yield much that would be helpful in approaching Ramirez. As it turned out, though, I learned a lot about the basic philosophy of satanism. I also familiarized myself with many symbols and charms that are used by satanic followers to communicate with one another.

I even went so far as to rent a video called *Faces of Death*. The film shows actual footage of a man being sacrificed in a ritual conducted by a group of satanists in Texas. These people recorded their gruesome acts and were eventually arrested for their crime.

Watching that film was a *big* mistake. As soon as the first scene came on the screen, I began to feel nauseous. I'd naively thought that because I'd seen so many horror films, watching the real thing would be no big deal. I was wrong.

About halfway through the tape I started to feel even more queasy, so I went into the bathroom to throw some cold water on my face.

"Jason! Jason! Are you okay?" It was my brother shaking me.

"Um." That was all I could get out. Somehow I'd passed out on the floor.

"Jason, what happened?"

"I don't know," I said, genuinely confused. "I had a headache." I stopped to sip some water. "I went to get some aspirin. I don't remember anything after that."

"Jeez," my brother said. "I thought you were dead or something. You looked so still lying on the floor."

I could tell he was really worried about me. "I'm okay now," I reassured him, not at all certain that was the case. "Just help me up." This was *so* embarrassing, just like the time in elementary school I'd fainted in the middle of dissecting the frog.

25

Weak Stomach

I realize it's odd that I have this fascination with serial killers yet suffer from such a weak stomach. People sometimes ask me—at least the honest ones do—whether I might be a potential killer myself. I hear that a lot. While I freely acknowledge that what these predators do arouses my curiosity, let me be clear on this: there's no way I could participate in such violence against others. I suppose that's why I delve into the area vicariously. Like most people, I'm intrigued by what I don't understand.

When I studied the crimes of people like Ramirez from a distance, the thrill was similar to watching a good film; there was the shudder of watching something horrible unfold but also the comfort of pretending it was all made up. What Ramirez and the others did was "out there somewhere." It wasn't real. Mostly, it was just something I encountered in black and white in the pages of a true-crime book—or later, in the matter-of-fact correspondence of various Death Row inmates. But when I saw actual footage of what these people really did, how they butchered their victims . . . well, I nearly called off my project right then and there.

Eventually, though, the images faded and my intense curiosity returned.

In composing my first letter to Ramirez, I tried to get him to see the two of us as comrades—"men of Satan"—who shared the same interests and goals. I realized how frustrating it must be for Ramirez and other killers to be locked away, waiting for their executions, unable to act out their violent urges and brutal fantasies. I figured they yearned for what I appeared to be, someone who not only validated their lives but also offered a means to continue their depravity.

My thoroughly over-the-top letter to the Night Stalker read as follows:

Dear Richard,

How are ya? My name is Jason and I'm a huge fan of yours. I worship the Dark Lord too, and I shed and drink the blood of a sheep every night in the Dark One's name. I'm the grand priest of a cult here in Vegas, and all of my 57 members worship you almost as much as we do the Dark Lord. How are they treating you in prison? You should be free to shed the innocent blood of the lamb with us.

My people and I would really appreciate it if you could give us some words or teachings to help us all follow in the path you've set forth for us. I have many women here for you. I will send you some photos of some if you

like. They love you, Richard. My girlfriend
wants you to beat the fuck out of her. She
wants you to show her what it is like to worship the Dark Lord. Please, if you need anything let me know. I will help you all I can.
[I drew a pentagram here in red ink.]

Hail Satan, Hail Richard,
Your loyal follower,
Jason Moss

In his response, Ramirez wrote a simple letter asking me
how I was doing, what Nevada was like, how old I was, and
whether I had any family. He also asked me to send some
photos of some of the women in my group, as well as some
"hardcore Asian bondage magazines."

It would take a bit of work to satisfy his requests. I had
one friend, though, who I thought might be of some help.

"Nando," I said to him, "you've got all these friends
who're models. You got any pictures of them?"

"Why?" he said, smiling. "You want to beat off or something?"

"Yeah, right," I said, laying the testosterone on thick.
"Like I can't get the real thing whenever I want."

"Sure, chico," he answered suspiciously, "so why you
want pictures of my friends?"

I couldn't exactly tell him that the Night Stalker was
fresh out of snapshots to masturbate over, so I told him I
had a pen pal in Europe who was a virgin. I explained that
he especially liked Latin women, so I thought he'd get a
thrill out of seeing some of our local beauties. It was a weak

story, I know, but Nando was a good friend who owed me a favor.

Once I gathered together the photos and magazines, I sent the package off to Ramirez and crossed my fingers. I didn't have to wait long.

In his next letter to me, Ramirez enclosed an outline of his hand. If I put my own hand inside his, each one of his fingers extended at least an inch longer than my own. It was huge—truly, the hand of a monster. To think that these five digits were responsible for countless rapes and murders chilled me.

Equally disturbing was his choice of stationery. Along the bottom was a row of skeletons holding hands. Written on the sides of the drawing were the words "Hands of Doom and Gloom" and "Evil Hands are Happy Hands."

It was apparent from what Ramirez had to say that he felt absolutely no remorse for what he'd done; he was actually *proud* of his terror spree.

"Death," he said, "is more than a word or action that takes place. There's no word for it. It's a feeling. One of immense, intense and delicious nature. Everyone cries. But death is good."

I was probably right in guessing that Ramirez would see me as a tool for evil, because he invited me to see him at the earliest opportunity. He warned me, though, that there was a wait to get in the prison and I could expect a fair amount of hassle.

While I was considering how I'd fit all these prison visits into my school schedule, Ramirez brought up the subject again: "I'll probably be in SF [San Francisco] jail sometime next year. Maybe you can come there then. Do I have your phone number? Have you ever sent it?"

At this point I'd been talking to Gacy more and more frequently and it was taking its toll on me. There was no way I could handle two of these guys at the same time. As it was, I felt surrounded by murderers. And while in the past I'd always assumed this project of mine would be relatively safe, when it came to my mental outlook, I couldn't have been more wrong.

I started having a recurring dream that Ramirez and I were both walking through my neighborhood, just talking and hanging out. I remember thinking that I should be afraid of him, yet I felt relaxed in his presence, like he was a longtime friend. In the dream it was sunny outside. All of a sudden, a young girl crossed our path on a bike. The next thing I knew, the whole sky turned very dark, then a blood red.

Ramirez smiled at me. "Let's go, Jason," he said calmly. I stood there, motionless, unable to move. I could only watch what Ramirez did next. He pulled the girl off the bike and held her down on the ground by her throat.

"Jason," he yelled at me. "Jason! Get the hell over here. Help me kill this bitch."

He began violently choking her with his gigantic hands, a maniacal grin on his face. "This should be fun for you!" he goaded. "Don't tell me you're all talk. You said you've done this before. Kill her!"

He looked directly into my eyes, waiting patiently for me to join him in his killing frenzy. When I hesitated, he began to squeeze the little girl harder. She squirmed and screamed, digging her nails into his arms. She looked toward me for help but I just stood there watching.

I tried to run away but I was frozen to the spot, unable to move, to speak, to act, to do anything but play the helpless spectator. I could do nothing to save this little girl. I was too afraid and powerless to help.

The next thing I knew, Ramirez was pointing a gun at my head. He repeatedly screamed, "You are not one of us! *You* are not one of us! You are going to *die*!"

Two or three nights a week, for a period of months, I would awaken from this dream, drenched in sweat. I was completely disoriented, unable to sort out what was real, whether any of this had really happened. Sometimes it was Ramirez who would see through me; at other times Gacy, Manson, or Dahmer. In every case, I would suffer terribly for my betrayal.

Some nights, I can remember the sound of Gacy's voice, calling out to me from a long prison corridor. "Jaaaa-son . . . Jaaaason." It would continue: "I see you. I am watching you. Come to me . . . ha ha ha. Don't worry, boy, I will just come to you . . ."

I remember almost being able to make out the face of the figure who stood at the end of the hall. Hearing the echoes of my name, and the creepy sound of babies crying in the background, I'd soon awaken and not sleep again for the rest of the night.

26

Grooming a Killer

If there was no respite during the night, the days were far worse. Gacy was pushing me for more and more attention, making more bizarre demands. Ramirez, as well, was hungry to meet me and kept asking for my phone number. I was able to put him off by telling him I didn't have a phone.

Meanwhile, my family and friends noticed the strain I was under. At times I appeared vacant and distracted; more disturbing were my overreactions to things that seemed quite ordinary to others.

One evening I was sitting in a movie theater with Jarrod, waiting for the film to begin. It's common in Las Vegas theaters to scan the audience, since there are frequent sightings of our more famous citizens such as Andre Agassi, Mike Tyson, or Wayne Newton. As I was making my usual survey, I noticed one strange-looking man sitting by himself. He caught my attention because there was a black bag placed protectively between his legs under the seat. I also noticed that he was looking carefully around the theater, which seemed suspicious to me even though I was doing the same thing.

"Jarrod," I whispered, "look at that guy over there." I nodded my head in the man's direction.

My brother briefly glanced over his shoulder, then resumed eating his popcorn.

"Jarrod!" I said more urgently. "Look, he's checking everyone out who walks into the theater."

"So what?" he mumbled with his mouth full, rooting around in the box for another handful of popcorn. "What's the big deal?"

"Look at the bag he's got on the floor. I swear, there's something real weird about him. I bet he's got a gun in that bag. Maybe more than one. What if he plans on opening fire on everyone in the theater?"

My brother just shook his head with disgust. "Jason, just chill out. Come on. The movie's about to start."

"Listen to me," I pleaded. "You know that I've been reading a lot about mass murderers and serial killers and I'm telling you this guy has the look. These guys have some type of anger towards society. They just snap one day. They want to take out as many people as they can before they kill themselves."

Now Jarrod was angry. I know I was scaring him. "Jason, he's a dork. He's not going to hurt anyone. He's just—"

The lights dimmed and the previews came on.

The longer I sat there, the more uneasy I felt. I could just sense that something wasn't quite right with this man. I had to do something.

"Jarrod, come on!" I demanded.

"What?" he said, really irritated with me now.

"Come on. We're leaving. I'm not taking a chance that

we could be hurt by some wacko. There are so many of these guys around. They could be anywhere."

I knew I wasn't making much sense. A part of me realized I was probably overreacting. But I'd been so immersed in the world of killers for so many weeks that now I saw danger everywhere.

When verbal persuasion failed, I grabbed Jarrod by the arm and yanked him up from his seat. He started yelling at me to leave him alone. People stared. I noticed that even the weird man seemed embarrassed by the argument. Jarrod finally gave in and left with me. He was so mad at me that he refused to talk to me for several days afterward. I realized then how much these killers were getting to me. Whereas previously I'd been getting enough out of the protracted dialogues with Ramirez, Gacy, Manson, and others to want them to continue indefinitely, now I felt an urgency to push things toward some sort of conclusion. If I didn't bring things to a close soon, there wouldn't be much of my mind left.

Although Ramirez had been putting pressure on me, I decided to give it right back to him; I was tired of being coy. In my next letter to him, I asked what it was like to be in prison. I wondered how he dealt with all the everyday strains. I wanted the reassurance that no matter how much I was suffering, he had it far worse.

"It's frustrating in here, for sure," Ramirez answered. "But even though I'm here, Evil lives in the world. As it should."

Then he signed the brief note, "Alive in the grave, R."

From this point on, Ramirez and I continued to write back and forth. In each letter I focused on a few questions I was curious about, all under the guise of being a devoted, concerned protégé who wanted to understand his world. Inevitably, he'd comply with my request for information, but always in brief, enigmatic answers that had the word "evil" embedded in the message somewhere.

Like any good behavioral psychologist, I rewarded him, each time he cooperated, by sending more photos of models who he believed were in my cult. He must have thought I'd discovered Lucifer's little black book, so numerous and gorgeous were the women I'd managed to conscript.

Of all the letters I received from Ramirez, the one I found most fascinating was written on his own letterhead. On the top of the page it proclaimed: "From the domain of the Night Stalker." In the body of the letter, he apologized for not having written in a while: "They took away all my stuff for 10 days. They accuse me of some bullshit. Thanks for the great pictures. She's lovely. You are lucky. Morals, scruples and all that other shit are just words to make people feel better about themselves. Enclosed is a flyer from a Satanic group in Florida. . . . Say hi to Jodie for me." (Jodie was supposedly one of the girls in my cult, the most beautiful model of all from the photographs I had available. I told Ramirez she was completely in love with him and hoped to one day meet him in person.)

The rest of this letter was taken up with diligent answers to each of the questions I'd asked him—he really was being most cooperative. I first asked him about the type of power he felt when he was taking the life of an innocent woman with his bare hands. To my surprise, he answered very directly: "The power is indescribable. But it's there. As for now, I can only fantasize. That's why this lifestyle sux. But out there, you can feel the draining of their energy, the total ecstasy. Get your mind into it. Savor it."

He included many graphic drawings in his letters to me. Sometimes the pictures were satanic symbols, or images of dismembered women. In one case he sent me a self-portrait in which he appeared as a manifestation of the devil. One hand is raised in defiance, middle finger extended, the numbers "666" etched on the palm. In another drawing he called "Trophy Collection" there was a mantel with a female torso on top. The body was severed in half, with both arms amputated as well. Blood dripped from the body, onto the mantel, and then into space.

Another drawing he did for me was titled "Breaking Up Is Hard to Do." Across the top and side of the page are the words to a song, "I got pieces of April . . . over here . . . over there," followed by musical notes surrounding the words. In the center of the page are pieces of a woman's body—a female head, torso, buttocks, leg, and arm—all severed and mutilated.

Since things were heating up with Gacy, I decided to take a break from Ramirez for a while, in the same way that I'd cut things off with Dahmer. My excuse for not being able to write for a while was that I was going to jail for beating my girlfriend. I felt that this was something he'd understand and appreciate.

In spite of my resolution to set some limits on myself, I was surprised how hard it was to let go of Ramirez. He'd been the most cooperative of all my correspondents, willing to talk about almost anything I asked him about. Yet as much as I was learning from him, I was paying a price with my own sanity.

There was no way I could keep juggling all these relationships at the same time. Gacy was the first person I contacted and I'd already invested a great deal of time and energy in that relationship. Moreover, he was becoming more and more demanding of my time. I figured that once I stabilized things with him, I could return to Ramirez.

In spite of this resolution, I found myself thinking again and again about the Night Stalker—about the opportunity he represented. Many times I thought about writing him again, but I'd restrain myself, remembering what happened the last time we'd been in close contact. Finally, my curiosity got the best of me and I wrote him again after a month-long interlude.

"Richard," I greeted him, "I'm back, and ready for the Dark Lord. I was in jail because I beat the shit out of Tonya, but that will not slow me down in any way. The urge becomes stronger, and our followers are waiting. I want to keep the letters coming again. I want the teachings to continue."

"Greetings," he wrote back cheerfully, as if our month-long hiatus was perfectly natural. "Thanks for the $10. It's been ages since I last heard from you. Say hi to Tia for me. So you were in the slammer. That's fucked. Did you ever get in touch w/Order of the Evil Eye? Ever heard of Hand of Death? Thanks for the two pictures. That girl looks like she's really enjoying it. Seen any good movies lately? Send more pictures of girls w/their butts in the air and back of their feet showing. To be sure I get them, send the pictures certified."

He really liked the idea that I went to jail for beating my girlfriend. In fact, this appealed so much that he immediately wrote again to get more details.

"What did you do to Tonya?" he asked. "Did you break her jaw? Did you stick needles in her feet and hands? Did you record her howls?"

I found this very disturbing. Was he truly wondering what I did to her, or was he subtly suggesting things for me to do to her in the future? I later learned that he was actually telling me what he wanted me to do to her on his behalf. I was now his implement of destruction.

He sent me the guiding motto of his life, urging me to follow this sacred truth:

> *Grant me the serenity for what I cannot change*
> *The courage to change that which I can*
> *and the wisdom to hide the bodies of people I kill*

If I wasn't aware of the number and exact nature of the crimes he'd committed, I might think that he was pulling my leg. But this wasn't Ramirez's way of elbowing me in the ribs, or winking at the mystique that had attached itself to him. He was *serious.*

To learn more about the way he operated when he was in a killing mood, I went the indirect route once again, letting him know that I was planning on performing a "sacrifice" of my own in the near future.

"What do you do right before you take the life of a victim?" I asked. "What goes on in your mind?"

"1st you have to be calm," he advised me. "Then, you savor the moment, you smell the aroma of the moment, the electricity, the blood, the beast." He closed the letter by warning me to be careful, to make sure I "tidy up." By this, he meant that after I finished raping and killing my victim, I should cover my tracks and destroy any evidence that might link me to the crime.

As I read this, I thought: What if I weren't a kid trying to learn from these killers? What if I were really a budding killer myself? Ramirez, Dahmer, Gacy, and Manson could supply me with all the motivation and ideas I'd ever need to carry through on a plan of total destruction. It occurred to me that there probably *were* people out there who were serious about carrying on the work of these deranged killers. If I could access this "network" so easily, why not them? It was an unsettling thought.

Shortly after resuming my correspondence with Ramirez, I was again feeling that I'd gone beyond what I could handle. The cumulative months of receiving letters describing Manson's insane views on the world, Dahmer's attempts at seduction, Ramirez's satanic visions of murder, and Gacy's sadistic sexual fantasies pressed down on me like a coffin lid.

With increasing desperation, a part of me groped for the sunlight, afraid that the old Jason might be irrecoverable.

27

The Experiment

So how is your weekend?" Gacy asked during one of our usual Sunday morning chats. These conversations had by now become almost routine.

"Fine," I answered. "Didn't do much. Had a report to do for school. Went out to eat with my family last night." By this time I was almost relaxed when we talked. Usually, about ninety percent of our conversation was about ordinary stuff anyway.

"Yeah?" Then out of nowhere: "How's Jarrod doing? Did he play baseball this weekend?"

The alarms started going off. "He's fine, I guess," I answered testily. "As a matter of fact, he's at practice now." Gacy always interpreted this sort of guarded response as jealousy on my part that he was directing so much attention my brother's way. I didn't bother to set him straight.

"So how is *your* weekend going?" I said.

"It's fine. I tried to catch up on some letters I hadn't finished. There are so many people writing me these days."

Was he saying I should be grateful? I wondered. Was this

a threat to cooperate or he'd cut me off? I thought about confronting him but decided it was best to just play along.

"Did you talk to Jarrod about anything?" Gacy asked in a tone that suggested he was winking on the other end of the line.

"No, I really haven't seen him much lately."

"Well," he persisted, "have you talked to him about the experiment we discussed?"

Knowing that the only way to avoid this conversational direction was to hang up, I tried to be firm: "No, John, I haven't."

"Jason," he prodded, "we've gone over this before. You need to slowly bring him into our way of thinking. You still haven't sent me any photographs of him."

"I know," I apologized, "I'm trying to get some. I'll see what I can do."

"Don't worry," he joked, "he's not going to replace you as my number one bitch. You know I like to be able to visualize who I am dealing with. I'm an artist, remember."

So irritated was I with having to keep up this charade that I said nothing. Gacy, of course, didn't slow down for a second.

"And if you don't hurry with those pictures," he said with a laugh, "I'm going to make you suck on my stick for a while."

After that remark, I ended the phone call immediately. I tried everything I could to change the subject, yet he still wouldn't drop the topic of my brother. It was apparent that if I wanted to maintain a relationship with Gacy, I'd have to make something up that would sound realistic enough to keep him happy.

A few days later I received a letter that contained a hypothetical scenario that was a thinly disguised blueprint for what he wanted me to act out with my brother. Every detail of this fantasy corresponded exactly to the layout of my house as I'd described it. As spooked as I was by how authentically he'd set the scene, I was actually grateful that, in a narrative sense, he provided me with enough of a start that I could follow his lead. Gacy's imaginary scenario between Jarrod and me went like this:

Late in the evening around 11:00, everyone had gone to their own rooms since each had a T.V. But we would tell the other to meet when the coast was clear. Both only dressed in a bathrobe, sometimes not even underwear as the robe covers it all.

One went to the other room and then they both descended the stairs down to the kitchen with no lights on and went into the garage where one would do the other. It would take 15 to 20 minutes or so, half hour if we both did something. And its wild fucking standing up, as all one has to do is lean over the car while the other raises the robe, spits in the hand and strokes the muscle then another handful of spit to the back side, and in it went.

I put the letter aside for a moment, not only to purge the sickening image Gacy was creating but also to quiet the eerie sensation that he'd invaded my house. The remaining pages read like what I imagine the *Blue Boy* equivalent of *Penthouse Letters* is. It was tough—*real* tough—to get through.

Gacy projected that my brother and I would eventually have sex three or four times a day. His own sex drive was so strong that this was perfectly normal to him. Of course, not in a thousand lifetimes would I even think, for an instant, of initiating anything like what Gacy proposed. But I had to "feed the beast," as it were. So in my next letter—fiction at its most blatant—I let on that Jarrod and I had begun to "experiment."

Once Gacy read *that*, a barrage of questions followed. He used disguised terms and code words referring to us so that he could deny any responsibility or involvement if we ever got caught.

His numerous queries actually provided me with the guidance I needed to create scenes that were sufficiently realistic and detailed.

"In your first encounter," Gacy wrote in his quirky, ambiguous language, "this took place with you being dominated by the other factor, and once the project was joined. What were your first feelings of what was happening? And as it picked up and discharged within, what feeling did you have for a first time? Thoughts of who it was and knowing this what were your feelings too?"

When I tried to field these questions, I discovered to my horror that I had to actually visualize the events as he described them. Mentally, the cumulative effect was something like sexual abuse. He was actually making me *think* of the most horrid, revolting sexual scenes I could ever imagine. And, in fact, for several months afterward I was totally asexual. I stopped having sexual fantasies and didn't think about sex whatsoever. This seemed to be the only way I could enter Gacy's world, or rather, allow him entrance into mine, without completely breaking down.

One technique I came up with that actually yielded a fair amount of insight into Gacy's habits was sending him two sets of letters, one supposedly from me, the other supposedly from Jarrod—both describing the same acts of "experimentation" from differing points of view. To carry off the deception, I used different levels of diction and different typefaces. Result: Gacy actually believed he was getting the stereo version of a brother-to-brother sexual relationship.

He reacted predictably—by writing to my brother in the most seductive way possible, feeding him graphic sexual fantasies in an attempt to bring him under his control. Of course, I intercepted all of Gacy's correspondence, whether it was addressed to my brother or me, so, thankfully, Jarrod never had to slog through Gacy's mental cesspool.

At the time, as stressed as I was by the burden of keeping up this increasingly sick deception, I felt a certain excitement that my efforts had served to cement our relationship. After hearing about my brother's and my "activity," he finally embraced me as his servant. He now believed I was completely under his control.

And in a sense, I was.

28

Hook, Line, and Sinker

I often wondered why Gacy, one of the most cynical and suspicious individuals I've ever known, so easily believed the stories I spun for him. While I'd like to claim credit for being a master storyteller, the truth is that Gacy *needed* my tales to be true. At this point in his life, he had nothing else but his fantasies—the letters I was sending him were his only reality. Later I learned from one of his acquaintances that he did in fact believe that everything I'd told him was on the level.

As far as he was concerned, he'd stumbled across an ideal situation, one in which he could relive some of his most deviant desires. He was writing the script, and Jarrod and I were supposedly playing the parts.

The one fly in the ointment was that his two leads were proving a bit difficult to direct. My character, in particular, kept balking at the idea of providing him with sufficient details of what we'd been up to. I realized that I'd made a mistake by giving him too much information too soon; now he was expecting kinky stories in every letter.

Since I was supposedly the inhibited one, Jarrod's let-

ters—or more precisely, the letters I'd concocted on his behalf—tended to be more vivid, and hence, exciting to Gacy.
But inevitably I hit a wall of self-disgust as I offered up yet
another dollop of titillation for Gacy's benefit, and at that
point I realized I had to change the focus of our correspondence.

From that point forward, the tone of Jarrod's letters became dry and tedious, mostly consisting of tales in which he
described encounters with his girlfriend rather than with me.
I didn't anticipate how frustrated and angry Gacy would become. In his next letter, he railed at Jarrod for regressing to
heterosexual activity and pleaded with me to bring my
brother back into line:

> Regarding J, I see his last letter was noth-
> ing again. Hey, if he is serious, then tell
> him to describe what he has been into or let
> me know when the best time to call where I can
> talk to him. But hey, he has to come out of
> his shell and tell me his thoughts, and what
> he likes. But this B.S. about sex with his
> girlfriend. Fuck that B.S. Thats for people
> who don't know better. He has got to know that
> I know all of his private instructions and I
> agree. But because you are not doing [it all]
> as often as you should, this is going to be a
> slow learning project.

After this initial scolding, Gacy sent along a typically
graphic and detailed sexual fantasy that he wanted us to act
out. The letter went on for pages, laying down a scenario

that resembled some of his classic killings. He wanted Jarrod to sit on my chest. He described exact positions he wanted us to try. It was Gacy the porno writer at his most creative.

I could only shake my head in wonderment. From my research, I knew that he enjoyed sitting on the chest of his victims, forcing them to perform oral sex from that position, often while he had a rope around their necks, tightening it according to his whims. Although he was a sadist, with young children he preferred to ruin their innocence first. Then, after they were "dirty hustlers," he'd begin inflicting the pain they deserved.

By late February and early March, Gacy had been denied access to Jarrod and his letters for several weeks. Finally, I sent another Jarrod letter just to calm him down. He responded immediately with this:

Hi Ho Bro,

Or should that be Lil' bro? Ha ha. Yes I know about your baseball as its your first love next to SEX. Please don't assume that I get mad at you as thats silly. Maybe Buddy says things too strong. And yes I would appreciate it if when you read my letters that you get back to me in a reasonable amount of time. Of course we could get over a lot of the letters by talking on the phone but you denied me that twice. What you have to understand in talking to me is its like talking to buddy. We three share a common bond and just like I have become Jason's big brother, he knows he can

```
count on me not to laugh or make fun of what
he tells me nor am I ever judgmental of what
he says. And thats the way you should feel as
well since I know just as much about you. . . .
```

There were a couple of things that struck me immediately about this letter. First, it seemed clear he was trying to join my family, to become the older brother who'd guide and mentor us. Although in this particular letter he posed as an equal to my brother and me, later he tried to exclude me from the "bond" we all shared. To him this was necessary because Jarrod required more specialized tutoring in the art of sadistic seduction. Gacy realized by now that the character of Jarrod was a far more willing pupil than the more reticent and timid Jason.

The second notable aspect of this letter was Gacy's apparent desire to train a successor to carry on his "work." If I was a potential victim—perhaps the last one he'd get his hands on—then Jarrod was a potential surrogate who could act out the things he wanted to do. The rub was, he couldn't bring Jarrod fully under his control.

When pleading and threatening didn't work with Jarrod— or rather, the Jarrod character I'd created—Gacy tried bribing him. As mentioned previously, this was one of Gacy's favorite tactics when he ran into trouble, and he favored the move even after he was locked up. In this case, he promised Jarrod one of his paintings if he'd be more compliant. By this time, he'd already sent *two* paintings to me, which I kept in my safe; a third soon followed that was intended for Jarrod.

It said something about Gacy's inflated opinion of himself that he considered the gift of a simple drawing sufficient to turn an intractable student into a worshipful disciple.

29

Q & A

As a way to encourage Jarrod and me to supply more details regarding our supposedly ongoing sexual experimentation, Gacy sent along vivid descriptions of various escapades he'd had with hitchhikers over the years. Many of these boys he eventually tortured and murdered, although the versions he sent me featured a lot of consensual sex. Tucked into each of these tales was a lesson concerning how to break down a victim's resistance.

The whole time Gacy was teaching Jarrod his tricks to dominate and abuse me, he was tutoring me as well—in the art of being a victim. In response to his insistent urgings, I'd begun reporting stories of hustling on the street—all, of course, spun out of whole cloth. He was very explicit in the acts he wanted me to perform, and what I should charge for these services. For example: for a "golden shower," in which I was supposed to allow a man to urinate on my face, I should demand fifty dollars. He also advised that, during sadomasochistic sex, if the guy started to beat me up, I'd be better off if I just went along with it.

I told Gacy I'd try some of this stuff—yeah, *right*—but

only if he'd agree to answer some questions he'd been putting off. I told him I was under a lot of pressure to finish a school paper I was doing on him and that I really needed his cooperation. Drawing on a number of sources, including the "fact sheet" he'd sent with his very first letter, I peppered him with a long list of discrepancies between his original confession, his eventual testimony, and the later explanations he offered to account for the presence of so many bodies beneath his home.

In two different letters written to me during the middle of February, he took the time to address each of the questions. In his introductory remarks, he seemed quite put out that I'd even consider the possibility of his guilt. He portrayed me as obtuse and ill informed, but decided to humor me anyway.

His ability to deny the most overwhelming evidence against him is evident in what follows:

> It is the totality of the facts on the fact sheet which gives doubt to my conviction, not just one thing. Thats why it was done that way. Thats why it is not me saying it but eight years of investigation proving all the points listed. Under our system of Justice a man is not guilty if the facts don't match the state theory of the crime or truth. Thats why the doubt is listed not with the major things but all the things which point to showing that this was a poor investigation of the facts in this case.

In a masterpiece of flawed logic, he continues:

The state said that I confessed to the Crime
and thats not true, so the state is presenting improper evidence. They are giving you
fantasy and not fact, which was told the trial
jury. That could have lead to believing my
guilt and that was false.

In my letter, I'd asked him point-blank about the manner
in which he killed the boys. I've read and reread his response over and over again and I have no idea what he is
talking about. He maintains he was framed, that the prosecution lied to convict him because he was a convenient
scapegoat, and that his confession was manufactured. He
then goes on to list every discrepancy and unknown item related to his case. Supposedly, if you add up all these incon-
sistencies, they prove he was innocent.

He cites, for instance, that the victims were killed in different ways, signaling different culprits; the police couldn't
identify some of the bodies, nor could they say positively
when the crimes were committed; there was a lot of drug
and alcohol use going on in Gacy's house—engaged in by
others, not him; the prosecution couldn't prove where he
was at the time some of the crimes were committed. His
main argument seemed to be that nobody actually saw him
commit the crimes, so he was within his rights to insist he
didn't do them.

When I read his long, convoluted arguments, all I could
do was shake my head. Did he have any idea how crazy all
this sounded? At his arrest he said unequivocally: "I did it."
Under interrogation, he revised his statement to say: "I
didn't do it; Jack did" (his alter ego). During psychiatric
evaluation, he admitted: "I may have done it but I don't

remember." At his trial he said: "Someone else did it and framed me." Later he admitted to me: "They [the victims] deserved what they got." Did he really think that other people were so stupid that they'd forget all the things he'd said earlier and ignore the mountain of evidence? In a word: yes. He concluded his first mid-February letter with this point:

> . . . if I were as guilty as the State would like you to believe, then how come there is so much to my appeal and I am not dead yet? Clearly cases of crimes with death penalty conviction after mine are already dead within 6 to 8 years. Next month we go into the 15 year. As there is a lot of doubt in my conviction. The May 10th date is not written in stone and I wouldn't bet that I will die then.

Although I enjoyed drawing him out in this way, asking him direct questions just to see what kind of answers he'd give, he'd only let me get away with it on a few occasions. In his very next letter, he indulged me further by responding to each of the fifty-three questions I'd compiled from various magazines and books.

In directing questions to him, I'd tried to focus in on areas he'd previously been evasive about. For instance, there was a long-standing story about his being caught when he was five years old smelling his mother's panties. Experts point to that as the earliest sign of his sexual deviance. I asked him to tell me about his panty fetish, whether he preferred clean or dirty ones, and what he did with them. He answered by saying that he used to take only the panties of his mother and keep them in a brown paper bag. He couldn't recall ever wearing or smelling them, and he said he eventually grew out of the habit.

I asked him about his voluntary confession to the police in which he not only admitted that he'd killed the boys but actually drew a map showing where the bodies were buried in their exact positions. He insisted that there'd been an illegally obtained confession and that the map must have been drawn by the police to frame him.

I was feeling more and more frustrated by these programmed answers until I came to a question concerning his being sexually molested as a child. For a change, his answer was direct and to the point:

```
     Yes [I was molested] by a contractor who
would come take me for rides. I was 8 years
old and we always ended up with him holding my
head between his legs. Until one day I was
hiding when he came by and Mom asked me why I
didn't go. After explaining, she told my Dad.
Next time this guy came by, my dad yelled at
him and he never came back again.
```

Gacy seemed to be in incredible denial about other issues, though. When I asked what it felt like to be beaten and abused by his dad, he vehemently denied that he felt anything but love for his father. He was equally insistent that all the other stories about him were false—that when he worked in a mortuary he hadn't had sex with the bodies and that he'd never raped anyone.

It was my very last question to him, number 53, that he seemed to find most provocative. I asked why he tried to make a point to outsmart teenage boys. He responded like this:

> I disagree about outsmarting boys, as they
> nowadays are streetwise. There you have the
> rest of your questions. You can learn all you
> want on the visit, as I will give you private
> lessons if you really want to know.

Now, *that* was a frightening thought. Until this moment, the idea of visiting Gacy in prison sounded like a novel way to spend my spring break. It hadn't occurred to me that he might be planning something special for me; after all, I'd be safe behind glass partitions . . . and everything would be carefully monitored by guards and video cameras. How creative could he get?

But there it was: the first clue that everything might not be as it seemed.

30

The Invitation

Every time I asked Gacy something that he thought was too personal, private, or confidential to be discussed over the phone or via the mail, he'd say, "When you come and visit, we'll discuss it then."

I just thought this was his way of avoiding having to answer. I also knew that I had neither the time nor the money to travel that far. In fact, in my whole life I'd only been on one major trip out of the state.

Additionally, there was the obvious problem of getting my parents, especially my mother, to agree to such a preposterous adventure. Many of my friends were planning trips during spring break to the beaches in Southern California and Mexico or to the ski slopes in Utah. I could just imagine telling my mom: "Guess where I'm going over the holiday? Death Row!"

At first, Gacy countered my reluctance by telling me I could hitchhike to Illinois, or even drive my own car. When, in a phone conversation with him one day, I balked at this suggestion, he said, "Don't worry. Let me see what I can do."

I started to protest that I didn't have any money when he impatiently interrupted.

"Look, I'll talk to my attorney. I'll have him send you a check to cover the tickets and hotel, even some spending money while you're here. How would that be?"

I was speechless. I'd now run out of excuses. I was also amazed that he wanted to see me so much he'd *pay* me to visit.

"Wow, John, I can't believe it," I said, really meaning it. "I'm actually going to be able to visit you. This is gonna be great. This is going to be awesome."

Now, how was I ever going to get my parents to let me go?

"Mom," I said excitedly not a minute later, "I just got off the phone with Gacy." I could barely catch my breath. "He said I could *visit* him. He said he'd pay for the whole thing! Can you believe it?"

"No, Jason, I can't believe it." Then she gave me her look that said I was being hopelessly naive. "What does this guy expect from you?"

"Nothing, Mom. He's in prison locked up, with no normal people to talk to. I'm his way of connecting with the outside world. I'm his audience." I could see her smirking, but I tried to ignore her and explain myself—a difficult proposition because even *I* wasn't sure why I needed to do this.

"C'mon, Mom, I just want to know what makes him tick. And this could help someday when I try to get into graduate school."

She rolled her eyes.

"It's the opportunity of a *lifetime*," I pleaded. "How many people can say they interviewed a serial killer?"

That piqued her interest. Every mother likes to brag about her kids.

She thought for a minute while I paced back and forth. "Yeah," she agreed, "it would be interesting, but I don't understand what a fifty-year-old man has in common with an eighteen-year-old boy. People don't give anything for nothing, Jason. *You* know that better than anyone."

She was referring to my constant suspiciousness. I was always assessing people's motives, and it was difficult for me to believe that anyone would do anything that wasn't self-serving. Looking back on it later, I'd find my making an exception of Gacy especially ironic.

"We get along great," I assured her. "The guy is just lonely or something and he appreciates the attention I give him. Besides, you know me—I can get along with people of any age."

When I saw her nod her head in agreement, I knew I was scoring some points.

"Besides," I said, spreading the frosting on the cake, "I could write some really cool papers for school about the prison system and serial killers. It's totally safe."

It was the safety issue that most concerned my mother, as it would any parent. There was no way she was going to let me go unless she was totally convinced nothing bad could happen. She absolutely insisted on talking to the prison's warden to go over arrangements for the visit and hear his own assurances that I'd be protected. I agreed this was a sensible precaution.

Frankly, I was amazed she was so amenable to the idea. I wasn't sure if she thought the whole thing was a scam by Gacy that would never come to pass. More likely, she saw, in me, a chance to vicariously live out her own fantasies of being a criminal investigator. After all those years of reading crime books, she realized how unique this opportunity actually was.

Now that my mother was on board, I knew my father would be a snap. The only obstacle was setting up a conversation with the warden.

The next time Gacy called, he was more than happy to speak with my mother, telling her that he and I would just hang out like old friends for a couple of days. He reassured her that he was just a regular guy. Sure, maybe he'd killed a few dozen boys my age, here and there, but he could be charming when he wanted to be.

Despite his breezy claims, my mother asked him straight out, "Look, you're on Death Row. What's to stop you from harming my son, or making sexual advances towards him, or even killing him?"

That seemed to give him something to ponder because he waited awhile before he responded. Finally, he said, "First, I've never killed anyone. Second, if I did hurt your son in any way, they'd take away all my privileges." He forgot to mention, however, that his scheduled execution date was just weeks away and he really had very little left to lose.

Still unconvinced, my mother said she'd have to talk to the warden, too.

"No problem," said Gacy. "It's already been arranged—hold on."

While my mother was waiting to be connected to the warden's office, I told her that because Gacy was such a prison celebrity, there was even more than the usual amount of security to make sure nothing unpredictable would occur.

Before she could answer, the warden came on the line.

"Hello, Mrs. Moss," he said, "how can I help you?"

"Well, Warden, my son was thinking about going down there to visit Gacy. How can I be sure that nothing bad will happen to him?"

"Well, you can never be completely sure about anything, Mrs. Moss. But we take a lot of safety precautions here at Menard."

"Will Gacy be able to touch Jason or be near him?"

"No, that won't be possible. They're each seated in two different rooms, with a glass wall between the inmate and visitor so they can speak to one another. Gacy will have his hands and legs shackled as well. There's also a camera in the room where the visitor is seated. This is monitored at all times."

"Really?" my mother said, apparently impressed.

"There's not much to worry about," said the warden. "There hasn't been an incident here in many, many years. Your son will be fine."

"Yes," my mother agreed. She seemed a bit flattered that someone with this much authority was treating her with such respect.

"Gacy gets visitors here all the time," he explained. "He's getting old, and surprisingly, he can actually be fun sometimes. I don't think a guy trying to get out on appeal would risk his whole life and the postponement of his execution to try something stupid. And let me reassure you again, all he could do is *try*. The security is just too tight."

Before my mother hung up, she hit the warden with one last question: "What about guards? There'll be guards around, right?"

"Oh yes, there'll be a guard walking the halls every couple of minutes, checking on Gacy and your son. If anything happens, all he'd have to do is holler, and a guard would be there in five seconds."

Thus reassured, she hung up the phone with a big smile, proud of how well she'd handled herself. She now realized that extraordinary security measures would be taken to make certain I'd be safe at all times.

There was one tiny problem with the scenario. The warden, you see, wasn't really the warden. Gacy later admitted to me that he'd gotten one of the guards he'd befriended to pretend to be the warden so my parents would feel reassured.

To tell you the truth, I suspected something funny might be going on, but there was no way I was going to say anything and ruin this opportunity. Even if everything wasn't set up as Gacy's "warden" said it would be, I was confident I could handle a fat old man in handcuffs.

None of us were really aware of the extent to which Gacy had a firm hold on the prison and its staff. He was a rich man by prison standards and could basically bribe anyone to do anything. He'd been living on Death Row for fifteen years, much of that time spent in the company of prison guards he'd befriended. Thus, he was fully in control of his environment, more like a celebrated guest than a convicted murderer.

And he had all the time in the world to plan exactly what he wanted to do to me.

31

FBI

Federal Bureau of Investigation," the receptionist said in a voice that sounded like someone's grandmother.

"Hello," I said. "I was wondering if you had anyone in your office who deals with serial killers?"

"Excuse me?"

"I'm a student at the university and I'm going to visit John Wayne Gacy during my spring break. I was wondering if you had an agent who maybe dealt with these types of people."

In a hesitant voice, she said, "Please hold one moment," and then I got the dreaded elevator-music treatment.

"This is Special Agent Reddy."

"Um," I stumbled, a bit flustered now that I finally had a real FBI agent on the line. "Are you the person I should talk to about serial killers?"

"Excuse me," he said a bit patronizingly, "but what exactly are you looking for?"

"Well . . ." I figured I had about one minute to establish my credibility or he'd hang up. "I've been studying and researching John Wayne Gacy, the guy who buried all the boys under his house?"

"Yes," he said, obviously bored. "I'm familiar with who he is."

This wasn't going well. I took a deep breath and just dived into the story. "You see, I've corresponded with him over the last couple of months and he's asked me to come and visit him. He thinks I'm this really stupid kid, and he tells me a lot of stuff. About his crimes and things. He promised me if I came to visit him, he'd tell me a lot more, things he's never told anyone. I'm not sure what—"

"Okay, hold on a second," he interrupted. "Let's slow down a little. I need your name and address, your date of birth and Social Security number."

I meekly gave him the information. I knew what he was doing. He was looking me up in the computer, probably checking to see if I was a known troublemaker.

When he got back on the phone, he seemed a little nicer. He asked me to tell him the story again, more slowly this time. He asked a lot of detailed questions about how I'd managed to strike up a relationship with Gacy and what I was after. Once I gained his trust, we had a good conversation. He even told me about his younger daughter, who also went to the university.

"I want you to call Special Agent Welcher in the Chicago field office. I'll call her first to let her know who you are and that you'll be contacting her. She's the agent who deals with Gacy out there, and she's probably the best person to help out with this. I'd urge you to make contact with her before you visit the prison."

After waiting half a day for Reddy to give Welcher a heads-up, I called the Chicago field office and spoke to her.

She was most cooperative and friendly, eager to hear my tale.

She asked me all the questions I'd grown used to: why I'd contacted Gacy and other serial killers, what I was going to do with the information, and whether my parents approved of what I was doing. Apparently, I answered correctly because she gave me the lowdown on what to expect.

"Jason," she concluded, "I'd like to debrief you after your visit and find out what you learned. Would you please call me from your hotel room or when you return home? If you need anything at all, or if something happens, feel free to call the office and we'll assist you."

"Thanks," I replied, genuinely grateful she'd taken me seriously.

"I really don't think he's going to give you much. I've been talking to him for years. He loves to play mind games. He'll try to control the conversation the whole time you talk with him."

"Yeah," I agreed. "I sure know that."

"Well, obviously if he wants to tell you about any of the murders, or others we're not yet aware of, I'd like to know about it. He talks and corresponds with a lot of pedophiles, some of whom we're actively doing investigations on. Any names or lists of these people would be helpful as well."

"Okay, I'll try."

"One more thing," she said. "He keeps a folder containing information on all his victims. See if you can get a look inside. We think it might include details we don't have."

I assured her I'd do my best. She then wished me luck and told me to be careful. "He's still a very dangerous man," she warned.

I hung up the phone feeling validated. It finally seemed

like the worthiness of what I was doing had been recognized. I realized, of course, that these agents were humoring me to a certain extent. After all, the chances of my learning anything of value were remote. Still, officials of the country's top law enforcement organization had heard me out—and had even been encouraging. For that I was grateful.

32

Journey

I'd never traveled much and this was to be one of the first out-of-town trips I'd make alone. My destination aside, I was pretty nervous at the thought of flying someplace all by myself.

I was scheduled to leave on a red-eye flight to St. Louis, arriving very early in the morning. Gacy's lawyer was going to meet me at the airport and then drive me the ninety miles to the prison. The plan was for me to spend three days in the local town, visiting Gacy each day for several hours. It was a lot of time with him, but I figured I'd need several visits to get the information I was looking for. Despite our three-month correspondence and all the phone conversations, I knew it would take a while to win his trust.

I spent the final day at home organizing myself for the trip. It was one of those early spring days when the desert winds were blowing. Dust and sand were everywhere. You couldn't even breathe the abrasive air without sneezing, so I was forced to stay in most of the afternoon and endure my mother's fussing.

"Don't forget your toothbrush," she nagged. "And it'll probably be cold in Illinois, so bring your red sweater."

"Sure, Mom," I said, exasperated. We'd been through this three times.

"Do you have enough money?"

"Yes, I have plenty."

"I'll have Dad give you some more anyway. Do you need your flashlight?"

"My *flashlight*?" I groaned. "Give me a break. I'm not going on a camp-out. I'm staying at a motel. Gacy set up everything."

She ignored me. I could tell she was really worried. "Do you have some books to read? Don't forget to bring gum for the flight."

Finally, to escape her nagging, and to vent my own nervous energy, I braved the winds and went shopping with my brother.

Walking through the mall, he and I joked about my destination. That I was embarking on this trip during spring break seemed particularly incongruous. Jarrod couldn't get over my chutzpah. "I think it's funny watching Mom and Dad try to stop you from doing all the crazy shit you do," he said. "I love to watch their faces when you ask permission for things. It just cracks me up when you tell them you want to talk to them about something."

I just smiled. It felt good to have my brother on my side. He seemed to understand how I thought, and he didn't judge me the way others did. Talking to him about my plans seemed like a perfect way to spend the afternoon.

Finally, though, the long day drew to a close. Everyone in the house was irritable and nervous, and I went upstairs one more time to make sure I had everything I might need to prepare myself for Gacy. This included a notebook that contained all the details of the stories I'd told him. I'd carefully logged the exact outfits I was wearing when I was supposedly prostituting myself on the streets, as well as the exact times, places, and scenarios of the encounters I told him I'd had with Jarrod.

I also decided to bring a notepad so I could "debrief" myself each day upon returning from the prison. I planned to take detailed notes on everything that had occurred, so I could re-create it all for the honors thesis I was already planning for my senior year.

In addition to the notes, pad, three days' worth of clothes, and a camera, I also brought along a book called *The Psychopathic Mind.* I was hoping to get some last-minute insights on how to handle myself during the visit.

Walking out the front door of my house that evening, I saw the worried look on my mother's face and felt a tinge of sadness. I realized how much stress I put on my family, and how apprehensive they were concerning this latest stunt. I was feeling pretty nervous myself, but there was no way I was going to show it.

A second chance like this wouldn't come along.

33

The Attorney

It was still dark outside at five o'clock in the morning when my flight arrived in St. Louis. I could smell dampness in the air. Smiling, I thought about how in elementary school we'd all run outside when it would rain because it was such a contrast to the monotonous dry heat of the Mojave Desert. It seemed amazing that there were places like St. Louis where the air was thick and humid.

At the gate I waited nervously for my ride. I saw several men standing around, looking like they were meeting people, so I tried to make eye contact. Gacy's attorney had a picture of me but I had no idea what he looked like.

It was about ten minutes—but it seemed much longer—before a man in a ski jacket and running shoes approached, his hair disheveled like he'd just woken up. I was very confused because Gacy had said his lawyer was tall and thin and would be wearing a suit. This guy was short and overweight.

"Are you Jason?" he said with a shy smile.

He seemed younger than I expected for someone who was an expert on appellate law. Actually, he didn't look like a lawyer at all but, rather, like a relative of Gacy's. He bore a striking similarity to John, with the same jowly face and body shape. They even had the same balding pattern. In a flash I put two and two together, sizing this guy up as not Gacy's lawyer but a relative Gacy had sometimes referred to who apparently functioned as a kind of all-purpose assistant.

"Yeah," I answered. "And you're Ken?"

Ken extended his hand, which I shook tentatively. He seemed confused as well because I was much bigger than he expected, not at all what he imagined a meek eighteen-year-old kid would look like.

He was a chain-smoker and he seemed nervous. I wondered why: I was the one who should be anxious—especially since Gacy had lied about sending his attorney. Still, he seemed friendly enough, eager to please and accommodate me any way he could. I was relieved by his cooperation because I was going to be dependent on him for transportation during the next several days. I was too young to rent a car, so the only way I could get to and from the prison was with him as an escort.

We walked out to the parking lot where he had a rental car waiting that Gacy had paid for. The sky was just beginning to lighten to a dark gray. Once again, I noted the smell of rain in the air. I kept taking deep breaths so I could remember what it felt like.

During the hour drive into the town where I'd be staying, I watched the scenery flash by. It was so different from anything I'd ever seen. Everything was so green and lush. We passed farms and little stores and grazing land. There were cows everywhere. I'd never seen so many cows in my life! Then it started to drizzle.

I managed to keep the conversation on Ken during most of the trip. I was trying to find out who exactly he was and what his relationship was to Gacy. From what I could determine, he was Gacy's "guy Friday"—someone who worked as a gofer running errands for the attorneys. Occasionally, he said, he even handled some of the legal chores himself. He visited Gacy on a regular basis, bringing him supplies, books and magazines, and messages.

It struck me as quite a strange relationship. Gacy later told me he didn't trust Ken much; he was just using him for his money and time. As for Ken's devotion, the family tie seemed to be the least of it. Mostly, Ken enjoyed hanging around with someone he considered a celebrity.

"Everyone wants a piece of me," Gacy later told me. "And Ken is no different. He just likes to be around me so he can tell people he's my friend."

I think it was Ken's docility and passivity that really earned Gacy's disapproval. I, on the other hand, *appreciated* those qualities in him. As you can imagine, I was quite apprehensive regarding what Gacy might really have in store for me. It was obvious, though, that Ken wouldn't be a threat. In fact, I quite liked him. That is, until we started to check into the motel.

"That will be one room, please," he said. "Two beds."

"No, Ken!" I objected a little too loudly. "We need to get *two* rooms."

"Jason," he said, almost whining, "John said for us to get one room. He was definite about that." Then as an afterthought, he said, "It's just to save money, if you know what I mean."

Yes, I knew *exactly* what he meant—or thought I did. My theory was that Gacy believed I was so poor, I wouldn't have any choice but to stay in whatever accommodations he'd arranged. He'd set things up so that Ken and I would be sleeping in the same room, knowing I couldn't object. Gacy had told his relative about my supposed sexual proclivities and what a handsome fellow I was. It seemed reasonable to conclude that Gacy's plan was to make a "gift" of me, and get back detailed reports that would enable him to experience vicariously what was beyond his grasp.

"I'm sorry, Ken," I said, acting as if I really was disappointed, "but one of my parents' conditions for my going on this trip was that I stay in my own room. They said they'd pay for it."

Well, the first statement was true anyway. As for the latter, *I'd* be the one paying.

Ken seemed quite dismayed. "You know," he pressed, "it sure would be a lot easier if we used the same room. That's the way John wanted it." Then he shrugged, as if to say: *Well, if you want to disappoint him . . .*

"Look, Ken, it's no big deal. But my parents would feel better if we did it this way." With that, I turned. "See you in a little while for breakfast."

As I watched him walk to his own room, I considered whether I should dump him and try to arrange my own visits to the prison. He seemed harmless enough, though, and I was grateful for the companionship. I felt very alone in this strange place.

The town of Chester, Illinois, was very small and quiet—like something out of an old movie. Coming from the hustle and bustle of Las Vegas, I found its tranquillity and beauty appealing. All the houses looked as if they'd been built in the 1920s. The bank, the movie theater, the stores—they all looked like antiques.

Apparently, the town's most famous former citizen had been the creator of Popeye, the cartoon character. There were statues honoring the guy all over the place, and once a year the town organized a Popeye celebration.

Chester was actually built around Menard Correctional Center, the town's largest employer. Most of the guards and their families lived there. Strangers were relatively rare.

"Whenever people come to town looking different," the girl at the front desk of the motel explained, "we usually assume they're coming to visit an inmate. You're probably here to see one of the big ones like Gacy."

Ken and I ate breakfast at a little diner. It was so quaint I wanted to take out my camera and shoot pictures. There was a group of older men sitting at a table, drinking coffee and talking. They kept looking at us, no doubt guessing at our relationship and which prisoner we were going to see.

"Don't worry," Ken tried to reassure me. "They're staring because you're so young. For entertainment in the mornings they all sit there and talk about the visitors. Just ignore them."

During breakfast he told me what to expect going into Death Row for the first time. He said I should leave all of my jewelry in the motel room because it wasn't allowed, and that I should try not to wear anything with metal on it, including jeans with zippers, because the metal would make the machine go off.

"This has been so stressful on the family," he said, abruptly changing the subject. "Having a relative on Death Row isn't easy. It takes a toll on all of us."

"Yeah, I can imagine it's tough on you at times."

"You don't know the half of it, Jason. I mean, John isn't

exactly easy to get along with. He's always asking me to do stuff and he gets kinda moody at times."

I felt sorry for the guy. He seemed to have devoted his whole life to taking care of Gacy, a man who had no respect for him and showed little appreciation for his efforts.

We finished our breakfast under the careful scrutiny of the old men and then headed for the prison. Finally, I'd have some answers to my questions, though not the ones I was prepared to ask.

34

Long Walk

From a distance, the prison looked like a medieval castle.
Built in 1878, Menard Correctional Center is the largest
maximum security facility in the state of Illinois. It houses
mostly long-term prisoners serving sentences of twenty
years or more. But it also counts among its residents those
inmates who're considered especially violent and uncooper-
ative.

As we approached the gates, I spied one very large red
brick building that I later learned housed the general popu-
lation. The building looked quite old. Massive fences surrounded the entire facility, fanning outward in layers. About
twenty fortified guard towers added to the feeling of im-
pregnability.

"There it is," Ken said as he pointed to a building in the
distance. "That's where they keep the most dangerous
ones."

I strained my neck to catch a glimpse of Death Row over
the barbed-wire fence. All I could see was the edge of a
quite ordinary-looking building, as old and worn as all the
rest. The building that houses Death Row sits high on a hill

overlooking the Mississippi River as it winds its way through Illinois on its way to the Gulf of Mexico. Although the state doesn't actually execute people at this facility, it does keep them in storage here until they're called elsewhere.

"Well, time for you to go," Ken said in his usual cheerful voice. Bless his heart, though. He could tell how nervous I was.

"So you'll be coming to get me when?" I asked. I wanted to make sure I had all the details clear in my head.

He took me through the plan for the fourth time. Everything would be taken care of. All I had to do now was walk through the gate.

I approached the entrance slowly, shifting my gaze from left to right as if I were afraid someone was about to pounce. A guard buzzed me through and then proceeded to X-ray me. He removed all my personal possessions and gave me a bunch of forms to sign. In essence, the paperwork absolved the prison of responsibility for anything that might happen.

"Two forms of identification, please," the guard said, eyeballing me as if I'd just committed murder myself.

I handed him my driver's license and Social Security card. "Why do you guys need all this information?" I asked, genuinely curious. "Do you get a lot of visitors here?"

The man just sat silently behind the counter, writing down all the information that appeared on my IDs. *Not one for small talk,* I concluded.

"Have you been to the prison before?" he finally asked in a bored voice.

"No, this is my first time," I said brightly. I added, "I'm

doing a project for school." I wanted him to know that I wasn't related to any of the inmates.

He looked down from his perch. "There are a few things that I need to tell you before you go inside."

I nodded and remained at attention.

"In the unlikely event hostages are taken inside the prison, we won't negotiate for your release. If something happens in there, if there's a riot or an escape attempt, we won't give an inmate as much as a pack of cigarettes for your release. If we did, then the prisoners would do it all the time, thinking they could get privileges, or even their freedom."

I couldn't believe he was telling me this. Even if it was true, why did he have to tell me in such a cold way? "So you're saying that if someone takes me hostage, you'd let them *kill* me before you did anything to save me?"

"Yeah, exactly," the guard said with a smirk.

At another checkpoint, a guard directed me to place all my belongings except for a watch and twenty-five dollars in a locker.

As I was cleared to enter, I heard another guard say on a walkie-talkie, "Get Gacy, he's got a visitor." At those words, my heart started racing. I looked back one last time, then entered a room furnished with vending machines.

This area looked like an elementary school cafeteria, but not nearly as nice. Blinding white cinder blocks rose up on four sides. Above, a seepage stain smeared the ceiling with yellow. The air smelled of old coffee and burned-out cigarettes.

I'd been passed along to another guard who escorted me inside. Leon was a small guy and really ugly. In addition to his slight build and acne-pitted, unshaven face, he displayed a short scar on his right cheek.

"Mind if I ask you some questions?" I asked. "I'm doing a project on the prison system for school."

"Sure, what do you want to know?"

"Do you feel safe here working with all these convicts? I mean, aren't you worried you might get attacked?"

"Not really. If you treat them right, they'll treat you good, too. If you treat them like shit, then you gotta expect trouble back."

"Like what?" I asked. "Can you give me an example of what happened to a guard who got attacked?"

He hesitated a second, perhaps considering how much of a raconteur he wanted to be. "Well, there's this guard who we call Leaky. We call him that *now* because he was dragged into a cell and stabbed eighteen times in the chest and stomach with a pencil."

"No *shit*?" I said. I wish I'd kept my mouth shut. I was just trying to keep the guy talking so I didn't have to think about where I was going.

"Yeah, he just got on this power kick. But he's a different man now."

"You mean he's still alive?"

"Oh yeah," Leon said with relish, enjoying the effect this story was having on me. "He still works here."

"Don't you think that's just a little crazy—to be still working here? I mean, is it worth dying for your job?"

"Nah," Leon said. "I would've left. I'm gonna be out of here anyway. I'm taking the test soon to become a regular police officer. Leaky has nowhere else to go. He's got a family, and I guess he's kind of trapped. He sure is a lot more laid-back now."

Leon pointed to the vending machines and explained that I'd need to load up on food for the day. Although even the thought of food made me sick, I put in some money and got a microwavable hamburger.

"Are you sure that's all you want? It can be a long day, and you might get hungry later."

"I don't have much of an appetite."

"Okay, then," he said. "Now stay close behind me."

He and I walked into an empty, windowless chamber. Once inside this steel cage, all conversation stopped. In fact, nobody I came in contact with during this long walk said a single word to me.

As we made our way through the winding corridors, I could hear the constant clattering of prisoners yelling and talking to one another. Some hallways echoed with the blast of radios; others were completely silent. Even more noticeable than the noise was the musty smell. The whole place reeked of mildew and sweat.

The only prisons I'd ever seen before were in movies, and they didn't look like this. Despite Menard's worn facade, I'd entered this building expecting a clean and modern interior—but this was more like a dungeon. The stairwells were dimly lit and spooky. The walls and floors were dirty. And the air! It felt old and stale, like it had been recirculating for fifty years, retaining all the dust and dampness. I kept stifling the urge to sneeze.

Leon left me in another waiting room, until he could go around to the other side and open the gate to Death Row. If I felt self-conscious before, now I felt utterly transparent. Down the corridor, handheld mirrors poked through cell bars and tilted to capture an image of me.

After what seemed like an eternity, Leon finally let me

through the gate, where I was asked to sign in one more time. As I gripped the pen, I noticed my hand was shaking.

As I entered the long corridor, I was nearly sick with apprehension. My heart was thumping so hard in my chest I couldn't catch my breath. I steadied myself, trying to keep my balance. In less than a minute I was going to meet John Wayne Gacy, and suddenly the irony dawned on me. Despite exchanging hundreds of letters with him, despite speaking with him on the phone several times a week, I realized I didn't really know him. Until a person visited this place and saw what Gacy had been forced to put up with every day for fifteen years, they couldn't really know who he was—or what he might be capable of.

I was about to find out.

I gathered myself together, took a shallow breath, the best I could manage at the time, and forced myself to look straight ahead toward the barred door and the person who was waiting beyond it.

Gacy stood quietly and patiently as I approached. I noticed with alarm that his only restraint was a pair of loose handcuffs, fitted on him by a guard who stood by. When I drew even with the door, the guard opened it for me, and I stepped inside. He then stepped through to where I'd been, locked the door, and began to walk away.

"Ah, excuse me," I said, close to panic. Surely he wasn't just going to leave me here alone! "Excuse me! Guard!"

The guard turned around to look at me through the bars. I could make out a thin smile.

"I was just wondering where you were going," I said. This was *nothing* like I'd been led to expect.

He just looked at me, shook his head, and continued to walk away.

"Guard," I yelled to his back, "where will you be if I need you?"

Maybe he didn't hear me, I thought as I watched him round the corner. I couldn't believe I was being left alone with a man who'd killed thirty-three boys my age!

Just as I thought about calling out one more time, I noticed Gacy watching me with an amused smile. God, this was humiliating.

I was utterly speechless. I couldn't have yelled for help even if I'd wanted to. My heart was now hammering so hard my chest ached. I could feel little droplets of sweat running down my back.

At that moment, as terrified as I felt, incredibly, I also experienced a certain thrill. I'd done it! I'd come face-to-face with a genuine monster! Believing this meeting was the end product of *my* careful planning, not Gacy's, I told myself I was still in control. Some of my confidence came back.

I can do this, I thought. *I can do this.*

35

Face-to-Face

I was utterly alone in the visiting area, except for Gacy standing motionless in front of me, eerily still. Looking at the guy, you'd hardly think he was capable of such brutal violence. He appeared to be a short, fat, aging, jolly fellow—sort of like the slightly weird uncle you tolerate because he means well. He stood about five feet, eight inches tall and was extremely overweight. His face was chubby, with skin so pale and soft it appeared translucent. His hair was carefully combed and styled with some sort of thick oil. He seemed ordinary in every sense—a harmless man who wouldn't hurt a fly.

Without saying a word, he extended his handcuffed wrists to shake my hand. *God, I'm about to touch him!* As repulsed as I was, I also felt exhilarated. I put out my sweaty hand to greet his.

Rather than look directly at my face, he smiled as he held my hand and looked down at my crotch. That small gesture was enough for me to consider pulling away my hand and running for my life.

"Nice to see you," he said as he continued holding on to

my hand. I could feel his index finger gently caress the inside of my wrist.

As I opened my mouth to say something, he turned and began walking away. After looking back furtively at the locked door, I fell into step behind him.

The visiting area consisted of one large room, sealed off from the guards by steel bars. A small walkway led from there to several smaller rooms designed for privacy. Some rooms were furnished with a table and chairs; others were so tiny there was space for only two chairs. One larger room was designed for an inmate to speak through a partition to visitors on the other side.

I wondered why Gacy and I weren't meeting in the partitioned room as I'd been told to expect. There was even a video camera there to monitor everything. Before I could ask, Gacy gestured toward me impatiently.

"Come on, Jason," he prodded, "this way." Then he led me to the end of the hall, farthest away from the corridor where the guards were supposedly stationed.

He seemed to have arranged the room according to his exact specifications. The space was tiny, even claustrophobic, and he'd placed two chairs side by side so it would be impossible for me to put myself beyond his grasp.

The only other furnishings in the room were a radiator and a piece of wood that looked like it could function as a desktop if we both balanced it on our knees. Gacy's "logbook"—the one the FBI agent had wanted me to gain access to—lay on the floor. Actually, it wasn't a book per se, but a massive red file folder labeled "Top Secret Case Files." I'd shortly learn what its contents included: autopsy results for each victim, a copy of all of Gacy's appeals to the Supreme Court, and full documentation supporting

Gacy's theory that he'd been framed for the thirty-three murders.

As I took the seat Gacy offered me, I noticed that directly across from our room was a small janitorial room that smelled of cleaning supplies. I could see a mop in there, some rusty chains, a bucket, and a chair. The chair was the only item that looked as if it hadn't been there for a hundred years. In fact, it appeared to have been deliberately placed there. As I finished getting my bearings, the other thing I couldn't help but notice was that we were seated out of the range of the video camera that was supposed to monitor our conversation.

"How did the guards treat you?" Gacy asked as he took the seat next to me. "Were they okay?"

"Yeah, they were fine," I answered.

"I saw out the window," Gacy said, "it looks like it might be a nice day out today. Probably not as nice as Vegas, though, huh?"

I tried to muster some enthusiasm for this conversation about the weather but I was still trying to figure out why the security camera wasn't pointed our way. It looked like it might have been deliberately readjusted.

This whole scene was incredible! Whereas I'd expected security to be incredibly tight for my visit, I was now confronted with the reality that I'd be completely on my own. There was no glass partition separating us. There were no guards standing around monitoring the conversation. For some reason, they'd immediately run off, as if they were giving Gacy privacy to do whatever he liked. In fact, as it would become clear, that's *exactly* what they were doing.

Over the many years Gacy had spent in the guards' company, he'd convinced them he was a model prisoner. Further, as a man of financial means, he was in a position to do them favors. Throughout the time I was in Menard, I noticed how close Gacy seemed to be with the guards. He had nicknames for them. He exchanged jokes with them. At one point, he didn't like what they'd brought him for lunch, so he just sent it back and asked for something else. Incredibly, the guards scurried off to fetch his requested meal, as if they were waiters at a four-star restaurant.

Somehow Gacy had arranged for us to be completely alone during our talk. I assume he told the guards he had a "piece of ass" coming to take care of him. Would they mind terribly if they made themselves scarce for a few hours? He'd make it worth their while. Since he'd never caused them any trouble in the previous dozen years of his residence, they had no reason to mistrust him. Besides, the poor guy was scheduled to die in a few weeks. What was the harm of letting him have a last fling?

Gacy seemed thoroughly pleased with the way things were turning out. Not only were we out of view, and the guards out of range, but there was nobody else in the waiting area. The reality was that I was alone in a locked, un-monitored room with a psychopath who'd raped, tortured, and strangled many boys just like me.

Making my situation even more frightening were Gacy's mutterings. "This is perfect!" he'd say, or "I can't *believe* this!" I said a silent thank-you for the cuffs he was wearing, albeit loosely. Without them, he'd surely be rubbing his hands together like some mad scientist about to throw the switch on a fiendish experiment.

The more nervous I felt, the more Gacy seemed at ease. We chatted for a while about the most ordinary things, which I thought was just bizarre. Here I was, an eighteen-year-old kid, talking with a convicted murderer about hotels being built in Las Vegas, the most recent sporting events, and what the drive was like from the airport. He seemed especially interested in how I'd gotten along with Ken, and the comfort level of the motel I was staying at. I knew he was fishing for details about whether Ken and I had become "best buddies."

After an hour or so, I'd forgotten that I was with John Wayne Gacy, the famed Clown Killer. Against my will, I began to trust this man sitting across from me, even appreciate his charm and wit.

Calming me further was the structure Gacy imposed on our interactions. In a bid to impress me, he showed me a couple of letters sent him by different news outlets, including *Inside Edition,* asking him for interviews. The unstated message was: *Look how privileged you are to have "quality time" with me.* In fact, he'd set aside three days for us to be together, although I had no idea what we'd do with all those hours.

After showing me the letters, he got up out of his chair and looked around the corner, presumably to see where the guard was. When he did this, I acted like I hadn't noticed. I just continued to stare at the words on the page, wondering what the hell was going to happen next. I didn't know whether to lead or follow, but figured that since the role I was playing was that of a passive, potential victim, I'd act as helpless as I could.

Believe me, it wasn't difficult.

36

Jekyll and Hyde

As I continued to dawdle over Gacy's fan letters, pretending to study them intently, I couldn't help noticing that he was staring at me. Eerily, he wasn't watching my reactions to what I was reading. Rather, he was looking at me the way a predator sizes up his soon-to-be prey, as if to decide which part to rip into first.

Over the last few months, he'd been trying systematically to break me down, weaken me, bring me under his complete control. I sensed that was exactly what was going on now, a hunch that was confirmed when he glanced around the corner one more time and then proceeded to lash into me about how weak and helpless I seemed. I was startled as much by the abrupt shift in his tone—from friendly to angry—as I was by his words.

He sat up straight in his chair, chest fully inflated, and stared intently into my face for the first time. Looking into his eyes, I experienced the most intense, powerful feeling of emptiness I'd ever felt. There was no warmth, no humanness there. Rather, it was as if I was staring at something feral. It occurred to me at that moment that Gacy's mask had finally come down. Now I was seeing the part of him that he reserved only for those who'd never live to describe it.

"You're here with *me* now, Jason. I brought you here. You'll do whatever I say. You know that, right? Are we clear about that?"

I couldn't stop myself from nodding. "Sure, John," I said, gazing at the floor in a subservient manner. How much of my behavior was an act and how much genuine was hard to tell. Yet, my instincts told me to continue to behave submissively. I'd worked too hard to get to this point.

And besides, I remember thinking at the time, I'm younger, bigger, and stronger—and his hands are cuffed.

If indeed it came to a physical struggle between us, I was sure I could overpower him. Of course, that's probably what each of his victims had thought. His genius was devising ways to trick people into compromising positions where their superior strength wouldn't matter. Since he had had months to plan for this encounter, I was very foolish to take him so lightly.

"You *do* know how weak you are, Jason," he continued.

"Yes," I said, hoping to appease him. "Can I see what's in your secret folder now?"

I was trying to distract him as much as I could, change the subject somehow. Things were getting intense too quickly. And I believed my "mission" was to gain access to his personal notes, perhaps even get him to acknowledge and talk about his crimes. At the time, I had no idea that the most valuable things I'd learn would come from our own interactions.

"You know," he said, "I could tell you to fuck off and

you'd have no one! What the hell would you do without me?"

"Please don't do that, John," I pleaded, doing my best to appear frightened. Actually, I was feeling a little nauseous. The more he loomed closer, the more overpowering was his scent. In addition to the baby oil he used to slick down his hair, he'd drenched himself in some sort of sickly sweet cologne. To this day, when I walk through a department store and pass within range of the perfume section, my stomach turns if I catch a whiff of that fragrance.

It was more than his smell that turned me off, though. The whole time he talked, he played with his crotch, constantly rearranging himself in his pants. He'd obviously developed an erection as soon as he saw me, and he seemed to have one virtually the whole time we were together.

"You know, if I was a bad guy, I'd tell the cops what you do with your brother. They'd take him away." He massaged his crotch as he said these words. "You'd go to jail. Do you want to go to jail?"

"Why do you say things like that?" I whined. "You wouldn't do that to me. We're friends, right?"

"I didn't say I *would* do that. Just remember who I am."

"I *know* who you are, John. You're the guy who looks out for me. You give me everything," I added, hoping that might stroke his ego.

But he was just getting started. His angry, intimidating interrogation went on for about two hours. Toward the end, so conditioned had I become to playing the whiny, groveling sycophant, I actually started doubting myself. I began to lose my bearings, forgetting what I was doing there and what I was after.

Then, suddenly, he snapped out of his aggressive posture

and began joking around as if the previous two hours hadn't happened.

"So, did you have a smooth flight?" he asked charmingly. "Sit next to anyone interesting?"

I thought I was going crazy. I wondered if I'd imagined the frightening emotional beating I'd just survived. His behavior was so erratic and unpredictable he had me at a loss as to how to proceed. All I could do was mumble inane replies.

"The plane was fine. No problem."

"How about Ken? Did he take care of you? He can be so boring sometimes."

We'd already been over this once, so I wondered why we were covering the same ground. I think he was just trying to re-create a semblance of normalcy after having just pushed me to the limit. He realized I was in a kind of shock.

It had now been several hours into my visit, and thus far I'd been drilled almost exclusively on how extremely weak and useless I was. Once we'd both agreed on that point, Gacy began chatting about recent movies he'd seen on TV. Then he talked baseball. Finally, I asserted myself.

"John, can I ask you a few things about the case?"

"Sure," he replied indulgently. "You do for me and I'll do for you."

I wasn't sure what he meant by that, but I let it go. I decided to begin my own interrogation by asking him about his first victim, the only one he ever admitted killing. He claimed he'd picked up the boy at the bus station, brought him back to his house, had sex with him, and fell asleep.

The way he told it, he awoke in the morning to find the boy standing over his bed with a knife. After a struggle, the boy was stabbed in the stomach and killed. Soon after,

Gacy walked into the kitchen to discover that the boy had made breakfast for him, and had apparently walked into his room with the knife in hand to call him to the breakfast table.

"See," Gacy said, displaying his scarred arm.

I nodded. "Do you mind if I ask you some questions about that night?"

"What do you want to know?"

Just as I was about to reply, I heard the gate at the end of the hall open up, followed by the sound of the guard walking down the hall.

"Food's here!" Gacy announced.

We were going to have *lunch* together? I don't know why this surprised me. I guess it just seemed incongruous that we'd be doing something so *ordinary*. It was almost as if we were ensconced at the Hilton and room service had arrived.

The guard brought in two trays, each laden with something approximating roast beef—plus some applesauce, a glass of milk, an apple, and some bread. The roast beef was a greenish color and extremely tough. It also had a horrible smell. I thought briefly about the cold hamburger I'd bought from the dispensary earlier, but even the thought of that made me ill.

Our conversation ceased as Gacy began to stuff his face with the food. I couldn't do anything but watch.

"Go on, Jason, eat!" said Gacy, the perfect host. "This is one of the best meals we get. I ordered it special for you."

I smiled gratefully and began playing with the applesauce.

"So," he continued, "you wanted to know about the

Greyhound bus boy." He took a big chunk of leathery meat, dunked it in some gravy, then stuffed it into his mouth.

"Look," he continued between chews, his mouth working hard on the meat, "it was consensual sex. We fell asleep together. Then I thought he was trying to kill me."

"But he was just making you a nice breakfast," I argued.

Gacy seemed to be staring at me intently. Was he looking at my crotch? No, it was my uneaten food.

"Hey, would you like my lunch?" I offered. "I'm really not that hungry."

He reached over and grabbed my tray, digging into the meat with relish. With his mouth full, he returned to the subject of his first kill, but ignored the earlier point I'd made.

"He ruined my rug," he said, as if that explained why he deserved to die. "Besides, he shouldn't have tried to attack me."

"But he wasn't trying to hurt you," I reminded. "You knew it then, and you know it now." This was the first time I'd actually challenged him, but I'd been with him all morning and I still hadn't pried loose any secrets. I wanted this visit to have some value.

He remained calm. "Hey," he said, "you don't stand over someone with a knife while he's sleeping."

"So what happened *after* you stabbed him?" I prodded. He was sopping up the last of the gravy with his bread, and I was afraid he wouldn't be so accommodating once lunch was over.

"Let me tell you something, Jason. You can tell when someone is dead because he shits all over the floor. The kid stunk up the place. I dropped him in the crawl space."

I couldn't believe it! He was actually admitting that he'd

put the body in the place where all the other bodies were found!

"So if it was an accident," I asked innocently, "why did you bury the body instead of just telling the police?"

Now Gacy adopted the same pedantic tone I'd heard so many times before, as if I were some kind of idiot who was altering the facts. Listening to him could be infuriating, because his arguments always sounded halfway convincing. Only after you carefully poked and prodded at his version of events did his lies unravel. After listening to him for a minute, I decided it was best to leave the burial issue alone and hit another angle.

"How did it *feel* to kill that kid?" I asked.

He shrugged. "It didn't feel like anything. I didn't care. He needed to die."

I pressed him further. "Did you feel any power?"

"Look," he said impatiently, "I dumped the body in the crawl space and buried it. I felt fine. I slept fine. I was fine." With each assertion, he seemed more and more irritated. He also seemed more and more distracted, until I'd concluded he'd stopped listening altogether.

He rose from his chair and began looking out in the hallway where the guards were now standing. He seemed to be watching carefully to monitor their movements.

"Um, John," I said with a catch in my voice, "when are the guards coming back? They promised to take our pictures together."

He suddenly turned on me, his face furious. "The guards are on the other side of the bars. Do you know how long it would take them to get in here if you screamed? Probably two minutes. I could kill you right now if I wanted. You know that, don't you? I could take this pen and stick it right here in your neck."

He'd been standing behind me as he screamed this, so I quickly assumed a defensive posture. He just kept ranting. "You'd bleed to death all over the floor by the time you got any help."

I'd never been so scared in my life. Although I was physically more powerful than him, and although he was handcuffed, the difference between someone on the streets saying, "Hey, I could kill you," and *him* saying it was profound. Adrenaline—psychotic adrenaline—counted for a lot, I knew. Knowing that those hands were responsible for the death of so many others my age ate away at my courage. I realized, then and there, that in spite of my youth and strength, John Wayne Gacy could very well hurt me if he wanted to.

But he wasn't going to try anything like that just yet. First, he was going to attempt to break me down completely, reduce me to a perfectly compliant victim.

"I have a special treat for you, Jason," he said, leering. He reached down into his sock where he'd hidden a small packet of baby oil. Apparently, he intended to use this as a lubricant to sodomize me, considerate lover that he was.

He pointed to the chair he now admitted placing in the storeroom across the hall. "See that chair, Jason?"

I nodded dumbly.

"That's where I'd do you. They wouldn't find your body until all your blood ran on the floor."

I tried to appease him as best I could. I was thinking, *Now's the time to come out of your role, let him know you're not someone to be trifled with*. But the strangest thing happened: I was frozen in the character I'd pretended to be. It was like I'd become Jason the Wimp and couldn't escape. I couldn't seem to do anything but reassure him he was in control, that he really could do whatever he wanted.

In some hidden corner of my brain it occurred to me that I was getting just what I'd bargained for. I'd wanted to know what Gacy did with his victims just before he killed them.

Now I knew.

37

Breakdown

Gacy just stared into my eyes for what seemed like several minutes. After taking one final look to make sure the guards were safely out of range, he stood in front of me and told me to stand up.

"Why do you want me to get up?" I said in a squeaky voice. It didn't even sound like me. "I thought we could look at your logbook now."

"Do you *mind*, Jason?" he said petulantly. "Maybe I'd like to see what you look like standing up! I only got a view of you for a second when you came in." That wasn't quite true, of course; he'd been stealing glances at my crotch every chance he got. But I decided to humor him.

"Fine," I answered, rising to a standing position. I couldn't believe that a few moments earlier he'd been threatening to rape and kill me and now he wanted me to model for him.

I took a quick stride across the small room to grab the logbook and then returned to my chair, making sure I didn't let him get behind me again.

My pose of being genuinely interested in him—despite

his barrage of threats—apparently disoriented him, threw off his "game" temporarily, because he consented to give me a quick look at his book. The contents included notes on everybody who'd ever been involved in his life. I was particularly interested in the section on me, in which he'd recorded the times, dates, and length of each phone call, also noting what we'd talked about. It was almost comical, the way his keeping tabs on me mirrored the way I kept tabs on him.

As I was turning the logbook's pages, fascinated by the details of Gacy's life, I caught a hint of movement just outside my field of view. Somehow Gacy had gotten behind me again. Out of the corner of my eye, I could see his handcuffed hands raise up and reach behind my neck. His mouth was open and he looked as if he was in some type of trance.

I felt his hands on the back of my neck and I tried to pull away. His grip tightened, and, with the leverage that came from his standing over me and my being seated, he pinned me against the wall. Just when I was about to fight back with all my strength, I realized he wasn't trying to hurt me at all.

He was trying to kiss me!

In some ways, this infuriated me more. The idea of his putting his lips on me was disgusting. In one quick burst, I broke away from his grip.

"What's wrong, Jason?" he coaxed. "You need to relax."

I could tell he was confused that I was being so resistant to his overtures. He'd gone to great trouble to get rid of the guards and arrange a private setting for us to be together. He'd spent months fantasizing about how this scene would unfold. Now I wasn't playing my part.

"Sorry," I offered, trying to regain my composure. "It's just that you scared me, grabbing me like that."

By now, Gacy's libido was like a freight train hurtling down the track. And mixed in with the lust was ferocious anger. "You're so pretty, you little hustlin' bitch," he snarled. "You like to get fucked, you little shit."

I cast my eyes downward, afraid to say anything that would escalate the situation.

"You wander the streets hustling," he said, working himself up. I noticed with revulsion that he'd now taken out his penis and was slowly stroking himself. It was obvious he was becoming more and more aroused. "You sell your ass. You do have a pretty tight little ass."

What the hell do I do now? I thought. Unable to think of anything, I just sat mute, noticing as I did that my words and actions had ceased to matter much. To Gacy, I'd become an object now—a thing for him to sexually fixate on.

"You can't pull that hustlin' shit on me," Gacy warned, continuing to masturbate.

"I know, John. I'd never try to hustle you, because we're friends, right?" I tried. As had happened before, I hoped that by invoking our friendship I'd slow his psychotic momentum.

"Look at my cock, Jason!" he demanded as he continued pulling on his penis. He must have thought that the sight of him—fat, old man that he was—would turn me on, get me in the mood, as it were.

As if . . .

"John," I pleaded feebly, "come on."

"Did you hear what I said?" he screamed. "Look at my fuckin' cock!"

"Yes, John," I answered. "It's very nice." I couldn't believe I'd said something so stupid, but what *could* one say in such a situation?

Having apparently come to a decision, he pushed his penis in the direction of my face and ordered, "Get on it!"

"Quit fuckin' around, John. I'm not going to do that now." Would the promise of something *later* appease him?

"Do you know how many little shits died for this cock?" he asked. "Do *you* want to die for this cock? I should have you bend over. Then I can tear the shit out of your tight little ass. You'd like that, wouldn't you? You want me to beat you, don't you?"

His breathing was becoming more and more labored as he continued to stroke himself, standing up. His face was turning bright red. He looked like he was going to have a heart attack.

"Open your mouth," he ordered, "so I can piss down your throat. You should like piss. You're just a big pile of shit yourself." Then he cackled insanely. It was just like a scene in a slasher movie. Except the movie was real, and I was in it.

I continued assessing my options. I wondered if I should kick him hard or really hurt him with the chair I was sitting on. What if all I achieved was to make him more frenzied and unmanageable?

"Come on, Jason, get over the chair here," he said, pointing to the empty seat. "You'll be a little bloody, but that's nothing. A real man can take pain, especially from another man."

It was at this point that I completely broke down. I'd like to say it was an act, that I faked tears to win his sympathy. In all honesty, though, I just lost control. Some part of me realized that Gacy was showing himself to me in all his glory because he knew I wouldn't be alive to tell anyone.

"John," I gasped out now through sobs, tears streaming down my face, "you said we were friends. Why are you doing this to me?"

Abruptly, he sat down and looked at me with disgust. His erection had now wilted and he tucked it back into his pants. "What the fuck are you doing here? Just get out of here."

"John," I pleaded, "you know that's not what I want."

Incredibly, rather than saying, "John, that's the best suggestion you've made all day," I was obeying my internal programming—an inner voice that preached "success at any cost." I couldn't bear aborting my three-day visitation with Gacy without having cracked his "code." I couldn't bear the realization that coming to Illinois had been all for naught.

We were both emotionally exhausted at this point, and both frustrated because neither had gotten what we were after. Thankfully, our first day together was about to draw to a close and it was hard to visualize coming back for the second. Gacy seemed to sense my reluctance, because suddenly he turned the charm back on. All smiles, he invited the guards to join us and had them take several photographs.

I was just about to say goodbye and scurry on out of there when he took me aside and furtively handed me a pair of bikini briefs he'd stashed in his own underwear. "Would you wear these for me tomorrow?" he asked in a pitifully pleading voice. He then pulled from his sock a silver bracelet and handed it to me. He also mentioned that he had a new painting he'd give me the next day. His 180-degree shift threw me off balance.

Walking out of the prison that day, everything was a blur. One minute I was awkwardly thanking Gacy for his hospitality, the next I was standing in the parking lot waiting for Ken to pick me up.

On the drive back to the motel, I shared some of what I'd gone through. Ken seemed shocked by my story, but he couldn't have been too surprised because he took me at my word.

"*Please,* Jason," he pleaded. "Don't say a word about this to anyone. It could really hurt John's chances for an appeal, or a postponement of his execution."

"Give me a break!" I responded. "He actually threatened to rape and kill me! There's no way I'm going back in a cell with that lunatic!"

"But this has never happened before," Ken insisted. "Most of the people who visit him are older. They're reporters and lawyers and stuff and he's always been—"

"I don't care!" I said loudly enough to make him cringe. "The guy is crazy."

"You just triggered something in him. I don't know. You're just like the boys he killed."

If I had any doubts about where Ken stood before, I didn't any longer. He admitted his belief that Gacy had committed all the crimes he'd been accused of. In a way, hearing this from him was a relief. That meant I didn't have to play games with him. I could confide in him, even get his advice on what I should do.

We both agreed that all those years of being kept in his cell, only allowed visits from attorneys and some family, kept Gacy looking normal to all who observed him. Seeing me had apparently caused him to relapse, as if a day hadn't gone by since his last murder. What I took for granted as "John acting crazy" was a side of him no one had apparently viewed in fifteen years.

That evening, despite the terror I'd felt at the prison, the thought that tormented me was what a failure I'd be if I gave up. How could I face my family and friends? I'd look so . . . so *ineffectual* if I let Gacy get the best of me. I couldn't remember ever feeling as low. Here I thought I'd set the agenda, control the conversation, find out what I wanted. Instead, I ended up a basket case. A crybaby.

I called the airlines to find out about rescheduling my flight so I could leave the next day, but discovered that the soonest a seat would be available would be the day after. If I didn't return to the prison, I'd be stuck in town with nothing to do.

It was while talking to my parents later that I realized what a corner I'd backed myself into. I heard myself lying to them, telling them everything was just fine. I wanted so badly just to tell them I'd lost it, that this killer had terrorized me. I wanted to cry. I wanted my mom to hold me and tell me everything would be okay.

After I hung up the phone, I brooded about the reality of going back the next day. It would be tough, but what if I could do things differently? Maybe I could reduce the risk. Straitjacket Gacy somehow. Newfound courage alternated with terror. There was no way I was going to get much sleep that night.

Each time I closed my eyes, I saw Gacy moving around my room, rearranging things to his liking, just as he'd done in the prison.

38

Day Two

I awoke the next morning looking puffy and red-eyed, but also with a new dose of determination. Perhaps it was stupidity masquerading as courage, but I still wanted to "tame the monster." I'd never in my life accepted a low grade in anything, and I couldn't stomach the thought of flying home with my tail between my legs.

The deciding factor was Ken's reassurance that he'd keep an eye on things during the day, since he'd be joining us sometime during the morning to go over some legal stuff. An added incentive was the arrangement that had been made for me to meet another convicted serial killer while Ken and Gacy were going over Gacy's appeal process.

This time Gacy greeted me with a warm smile rather than a leer, behaving as if we were old friends. He was obviously trying to put me at ease.

"What did you do for the rest of the day with Ken?" he asked.

"Nothing much," I said. "We just ate dinner and walked around the town."

"Did he try to fuck you?" he asked. I guess he was still hoping his assistant would do what he couldn't—or hadn't managed to yet.

"No!" I said indignantly, playing the innocent. "He was very nice."

"That's good," Gacy said, not meaning it. "I told him to treat you like you were my son."

Right. Gacy made it clear to everyone—Ken, the other inmates, even the guards—that I was his property to do with as he liked. As if to emphasize the point, his eyes went to my wrist where I'd made a point to wear his bracelet.

"Are you wearing my other present as well?" he asked seductively, referring to the briefs he'd given me.

Since I was damn sure he'd never confirm one way or the other, I nodded. In actuality, I'd left the underwear in my room. I could just imagine what a funny prop *that* would be when I told this story to my family and friends. To me, this was all still like a movie I was temporarily living in. Eventually, the credits would roll, and I'd get to go home and deliver my review.

This time, per my new plan, I launched immediately into business to circumvent any funny stuff Gacy might have in mind. We sat next to one another with his binder labeled "Top Secret Case Files" balanced on our laps. Periodically, I could feel him trying to "accidentally" brush up against me, but I repeatedly pushed him away. It was such a strange feeling, reminding me of when I was in junior high school and was on the other end of such advances, ones directed at girls I liked.

For the most part, we were able to stick to my agenda.

We leafed through his book, page by page, viewing the dossiers on each of his victims. He showed me the autopsy report on each, as if he was proud of his handiwork.

"They all deserved to die," he explained. "If you lead the kinds of lives they did, something was bound to happen."

I just nodded, amazed at his ability to deny responsibility. He seemed to be saying: *Even if I did kill them, it was their fault.*

"They went out in the streets and hustled their asses," he pointed out. "That's why they got fucked over."

This conversation was so strange because we were both pretending we were talking about a mysterious killer who had yet to be found. Although his language would sometimes slip, he was careful to keep up the fiction of his own innocence. Once I acknowledged his lack of culpability, then he'd freely talk about the crimes as if someone else had done them.

"John," I asked at one point, "who the hell is the guy who killed all these kids, then?"

"We think it's actually a group of guys. Probably drugs were involved."

I smiled at the way he used "we" as if his theory of the case were the prevailing one. I wondered what would happen if I pushed him more.

"Doesn't it piss you off to think that all these people outsmarted and manipulated you?" I asked. "I mean, to think that these guys came into your house, used all your stuff, and then framed you for murder. How could you have not seen it coming?"

"Those fuckin' kids couldn't control a goddamn thing!" he screamed, as angry as I'd yet seen him. "Nobody framed me. They just got lucky and I took the fall."

He seemed to calm down of his own accord. "The state contends I was the killer, that I had all this anger and rage. Shit, I had no time to kill anyone, even if I wanted to. I was running a $300,000-a-year business."

Continuing through his secret files, we next moved to his appeals to the United States Supreme Court. I had a keen interest in the law, and I was fascinated by what I saw here regarding the intricacies of preventing an execution. Gacy, by contrast, seemed profoundly bored. I noticed that he kept looking at his watch, then glancing outside the room to check where the guards were positioned. Each time I noted his attention averted away from me, I checked the time as well, counting the minutes until Ken would arrive.

So far, I was encouraged by the way the morning was progressing—it wasn't at all like the disaster of the previous day. It really seemed as if I'd gained the upper hand.

Unfortunately, my optimism was misplaced, a fact that became clear when I noticed the pen in Gacy's hand. He kept playing with it. Still vivid in my mind was his threat from the previous day in which he described how easy it would be to stick the pen in my neck and let me choke on my own blood.

"So, John," I said to ease the tension, "tell me about the next step with your appeal."

"Huh?" he answered, not at all sure what I'd asked him.

"I said—"

"It doesn't matter," he interrupted. "Would you like to see the way I supposedly killed those boys?"

"You mean the rope trick?" I answered apprehensively, remembering having read about it. It *would* be interesting to see how he did it. I was feeling confident I could control him.

"Here," he said, "give me your wrist. I'll show you how it works."

I noticed now that he wasn't making any attempt to hide his guilt. Strange how he seesawed back and forth between indignant protests of innocence and outright admissions of being what everyone said he was.

The rope trick is what Gacy called his technique of strangling victims. First, he'd place some rope around the neck of a boy under his control—usually, the boy was handcuffed with his arms behind his back—and he'd twist the rope once. Next, he'd place a stick or some other object behind the twisted rope and slowly turn it. This method of strangulation enabled him to have complete control over the victim's airflow. If he wanted the victim to die quickly, he'd twist the stick several times tightly, but if he wanted him to breathe again, he'd gently unravel the stick. Using this method, he could take his victims in and out of consciousness as he pleased, enabling the torture to go on for hours.

Gacy took the pen in his hand and inserted it under the bracelet I was wearing, next to my skin. "Feel the pain this could cause," he said, smiling as he twisted the pen around, causing the bracelet to tighten around my wrist.

Just as I started to wince, he said, "Now I could have some fun; I really could." With that, he gave it one final twist, pinching my skin in the process.

And just as one hand let go of my braceleted wrist, the other hand grabbed my arm. "Do you remember what we discussed yesterday?" he asked in a menacing tone of voice.

"You mean about your case?"

"You know what I'm talking about!" he growled. He

then brought my hand down to the level of his crotch. You have to remember that his hands were cuffed together, so if he had an itch or something while holding on to me, my arm would have to follow his down.

With his other hand, he began to undo his zipper and pull out his penis again, just like the day before. As he did this, he tightened the hold he had on my wrist. I could see his fingers turn white from the amount of pressure he was exerting. I struggled to pull my arm away, eventually breaking free. I was so relieved that I barely noticed he was starting to play with himself again.

"Do you see this cock?" he said to me in a hoarse whisper. "Do you see the big head on my cock? I'm going to shove this big head down your throat. You're going to choke on this cock, Jason, until you beg me to stop."

His face was now bright red. I could actually see his veins bulging through the skin. He was breathing hard, moaning gutturally as he stroked himself. *Uh-oh,* I thought. It was yesterday all over again.

This time, though, he was having trouble maintaining his erection, and to raise his sexual excitement, he stepped up the verbal brutality. "Jason," he said, eyes riveted on my body, "last night I lay in my bed thinking about what I'm going to do to you today."

I gulped. The confidence I'd felt earlier had just about drained off. "Uh, John, maybe we'd better—"

"I thought long and hard about how I'm going to rape you," he interrupted. "It doesn't matter whether you want it or not, you're going to get it. After I'm done with you, you're going to lie on the bloody floor so I can piss all over your face. Seeing your blood on the floor is going to make me very happy." As he talked, he kept massaging himself, working himself into a full erection again.

During the previous night, I'd considered what I might do if he came on to me again, or threatened my life. I felt somewhat better prepared to fend him off, but I knew that a knock-down, drag-out fight or a sprint to the barred door to call out to the guards would effectively blow the whistle on this relationship I'd spent so long nurturing. There was even a chance that an altercation inside the prison would make the newspapers. Before I took the final step—a fight, or sprint, for my life—I wanted to make sure there were no options left.

"You're just a piece of shit!" Gacy screamed. "You're nothing. You're worth nothing. I could easily take care of you *just like the others*."

He said it! I thought to myself. He admitted he'd killed those other boys. Of course, a lot of good that admission was going to do if I didn't get out of this cell soon.

As if through a haze, I heard him continuing to scream at me, "Take your clothes off so I can fuck you."

"Couldn't we just talk?" I pleaded. "You're scaring me."

"I said take your pants off. I want you to bend over the chair or I'll make you."

Okay, it was about time I let him know who I really was. I could feel my own internal strength return as I tensed to kick him in his fat stomach, or better yet, right in the crotch. The fat pervert needed to be taught a lesson!

As someone once said, though: *99 percent of life is timing*. Weirdly—perhaps providentially—at precisely the point Gacy began reaching for me and I knew one of us would end up badly hurt, we both heard the sound of someone coming down the hall. It was the guards!

It was almost comical. Ken and his escorts were on their way and here Gacy was standing over me with his penis hanging out of his pants. Just as the gate opened, he sat down and zippered up his equipment. He was shaking and sweating profusely.

"We're here," Ken yelled out as he walked down the hallway, almost as if he knew he should give some warning.

The first person who strode into view was Andrew Kokoralies, Gacy's friend and fellow killer on Death Row. Next came Ken with a chipper smile on his face that quickly turned serious when he saw Gacy looking sick.

I *had* to get out of this room. I couldn't stand the thought of being with Gacy for another moment. I had trouble catching my breath. I felt nauseous, probably from the overdose of adrenaline in my system. I was also very, very angry.

39

Neighbor Down the Hall

Andrew Kokoralies and John Gacy became friends because they shared a taste for killing, and also because of their proximity as neighbors on Death Row. While Gacy's preference ran toward young boys, Kokoralies preferred dismembering women with piano wire.

One of the reasons I'd agreed to return to Menard Correctional Center for a second visit was that I'd been alerted that Ken would be meeting with Gacy that day to go over his latest appeal, which had apparently been turned down, and some paperwork needed handling.

To keep me occupied during his legal powwow, Gacy had arranged for me to spend time with his buddy. This was actually a favor he was doing for Kokoralies, since the guy almost never had any visitors, nor did he have contact with anyone on the outside.

Kokoralies stood before me with a sly grin on his face, which I misread as that of another predator about to share the spoils of the alpha male. I later deduced that he was just so lonely he was simply glad for the company, even if I did "belong" to another inmate.

One of the reasons I actually appreciated talking to this guy—other than the two-for-one aspect of bagging interviews with two serial killers—was that I could shed my artificially passive role for a while. It was starting to itch so bad, I felt like I might break out into hives.

Best of all, though, it gave me a chance to get away from Gacy, the sight of whom now made me furious.

At first, Kokoralies looked intimidating, very much the prototype of the muscular, imposing, psychopathic killer. Despite his short stature, he was extremely well built. He was wearing a tank top to show off his rippling muscles and tattoo of a heart with the name of some ex-girlfriend.

I'd been forewarned there might be a chance I could meet Kokoralies while I was at the prison, so I'd done my homework. Besides the things Gacy had told me about him in various phone conversations, I learned that "Koko" (as Gacy called him) was a different sort of creature than the Clown Killer. While Gacy was a charismatic leader, a predator who preferred to hunt alone, Koko was more like a wolf pack member. He was certainly every bit as brutal and dangerous as Gacy, but only when he had someone else to tell him what to do; he was a natural follower.

Koko had been convicted of eight murders in which the victims, all women, had been raped, beaten, tortured, then strangled and mutilated, their breasts cut off as trophies. Borrowing a page from Jeffrey Dahmer's book, the killers even ate parts of the decomposing bodies as part of satanic rituals.

In concert with three other men, Koko trolled the streets of Chicago in much the same way Gacy had just a few years earlier. Actually, there was a link between Koko's gang and Gacy, since the leader of the gang, Robin Gecht, was a one-time Gacy employee.

Gecht was once heard to remark that Gacy's only mistake was to hide the bodies under his house. Gecht said it was stupid, that *he* preferred to hide bodies in isolated forested areas. Given the gang's skill at dumping bodies, it could never be determined exactly how many young women Gecht, Koko, and their two partners killed during their two-year rampage. Some of the killers admitted to twelve murders, while one claimed the body count went as high as eighteen.

After they were caught, Koko was sentenced to be executed and was placed in a cell on Death Row near Gacy. It was difficult to determine whether their friendship developed because of their close proximity or, more eerily, because Andrew was actually a "second generation" killer who'd worked for one of Gacy's disciples. Whatever the basis of their relationship was, I was relieved to realize, after only a few minutes talking with Koko, that he was far more manageable than Gacy. In fact, he struck me as not terribly bright.

"How are ya doin'?" he said to me with an open smile. "I'm Andrew."

"Nice to meet you," I said, smiling back. If I'd concocted a "Koko plan of attack" before coming to the prison, it was all a blur now. I decided to just wing it.

As soon as we sat down, he began bombarding me with questions. "John tells me you go to school. What's it like? Do you live there? Who do you live with?"

He fired the questions so quickly, all I could do was just nod my head. At first, I naively thought he actually cared about what I was doing with my life, so I answered each of his queries carefully, telling him about the university and the classes I was taking. I was puzzled that he seemed to show little interest in the answers I was giving, but I was content to stall for time while he revealed himself.

I knew there was something he wanted from me, but I couldn't figure out what it was. I replayed the questions he asked me again, looking for clues. And soon I realized that, just like Gacy, Koko had a very distorted view of reality. For instance, his vision of college life was that it was one big orgy—students had sex with each other all the time, in every room on campus. Since I'm certain he'd never read a book in his life, except maybe a few pornographic novels, it was easy to see how he might have gotten that impression.

Once I picked up on what he wanted to hear, I fed him some tall tales. I told him how whenever a guy on campus saw an attractive woman, he'd just walk up and announce in the bluntest terms possible what he wanted to do with her. I led him to believe that this technique worked every time.

Koko's eyes were gleaming. He was actually salivating. Imagine that: thousands of girls walking around, strutting their stuff, inviting guys like him to have his way with them. I tried not to think about what Koko's way might involve, or I'd surely lose my concentration.

He seemed spellbound by my fanciful tales of debauchery on campus. He was captivated to the point that his grunts became cues, urging me to tell him more. He timidly asked if I wouldn't mind sending him some photographs of the girls on campus, and then proceeded to write down his address.

Jeez, this guy was so simple. It had taken me exactly thirty minutes to build up trust to the point where it seemed he'd tell me most anything. Quite a contrast with Gacy! As I had many times in the past, I marveled at how diverse people are—even serial killers.

When Koko confided how lonely he was, I actually felt sorry for him. He had no friends in the world except for Gacy. His family never contacted him. He rarely had visitors—none in the previous few months.

"So," I asked, "how do you deal with being locked up in a room for twenty-three hours a day? That must be hard."

He nodded and looked forlorn. "You just gotta have a PMA."

I couldn't help smiling. Gacy had apparently passed on his belief that it is important to cultivate a positive mental attitude—PMA. It was obvious that Koko, a natural follower, had latched on to Gacy, a natural leader. Although their sexual orientations were as different as night and day, it made sense that, even in a prison setting, they'd act out their instinctive roles.

Whereas with Gacy I'd learned to be careful and diplomatic, with Koko I was very direct—almost recklessly so: "What hurts you the most about being in here, Andy? Do you dream about the women you hurt?" I looked directly into his eyes as I asked these questions, keeping my voice stern and confident.

It was like a dim light went on inside his head. Here he'd been told to expect a passive, worthless, weak kid, a boy toy Gacy had reeled in, but the person he was talking to seemed very assertive. *What gives?* is, I'm sure, what he was thinking. What he actually said was:

"You're nothing like John said you were!"

"You're right, I'm not!" I said with more force than I intended. I was probably declaring this as much to myself as I was to him.

Koko didn't answer me at first when I asked him to tell me about the women he'd killed. He looked rather taken aback and intimidated—by an *eighteen-year-old*, if you can believe it. But that fit with his "follower" profile.

I continued to press him to talk about the horrific things he'd done. He looked sheepish, like a little boy who'd been caught with his hand in the cookie jar. Finally, he replied that his lawyers told him never to talk about the cases as long as he had pending appeals.

I looked him directly in the eyes and didn't say a word. I didn't have to. He sported a rather large grin on his face and said, "A guy's gotta have his fun, right?"

It seemed like he wanted to confide in me. Given enough time, I figured I could get him to tell me anything. I made a mental note to begin a correspondence with him when I got back home.

It was almost pitiful the way he reached out to me, suggesting we could be friends. Koko had mutilated eight women—at least!—and suddenly I began feeling guilty for leading him on. He mentioned to me that one of the first things he'd do after his case was reversed on appeal—he had to hope for *something*—was look me up so we could share a few beers. He wanted to know if I'd introduce him to my family.

That question really caught me off balance. The underlying question—the question beneath the question, as it were—seemed to be: did I really care about him, or was I just talking to him to entertain myself?

I wondered at the time, and have wondered many times

since, what a friend of Andrew Kokoralies was expected to do. Would he want me to be his new gang leader? Would we patrol college campuses together, asking coeds to have sex with us, and if they didn't respond favorably, rape and kill them? The thought of his walking the streets again was frightening.

I was about to answer the family question when Ken poked his head through the doorway. "John is ready for you now," he said.

It was time to crawl back into *his* cage.

10

Goodbye

Lunchtime again. Two more hours with Gacy before I'd be rid of him. As I reentered his cell, I was determined to maintain control, to get through the next session. Whatever he had planned, I knew it would be drawn out as long as possible. The pleasure for him was in *playing* with his victims, not in the actual killing. As long as he believed I was coming back, I was reasonably sure I'd be safe. I couldn't let him know that returning the next day for another bout of "Will he or won't he?" was out of the question.

As we sat having a quiet lunch, the scene seemed almost tranquil compared to the earlier histrionics. I decided to take the offensive.

"John, why did you do all that shit before? Why do you have to scare me like that?"

He ignored my question altogether, attempting to reestablish his dominance. "You know that fucking your brother is against the law," he said. "You could go to jail for that, and your brother could get sent to a home. Do you want to see your brother again?"

Here we go again, I thought. This guy is *relentless.*

When one kind of threat didn't work, he just used another. I took a deep breath and for the last time slipped into my role.

"Please, John," I begged with just the right touch of panic. "You wouldn't do that to me, would you?" My mind was suddenly racing with the possibilities. Although I'd meticulously documented all of my tall tales, I wondered if Gacy could create problems for me. I could just see the tabloid headlines: "Honors Student Caught in Love Triangle with Younger Brother and Serial Killer."

I realized Gacy had been building a case against me all this time, gathering leverage he could use if he ever needed it. The only problem, of course, is that he still had no idea that every scenario I'd spoon-fed him was fictitious. As much as I wanted to throw this back in his face, I maintained my restraint.

"John," I said softly, showing appropriate deference, "could we talk about what your life in prison is like? I mean, if you want to and all."

He explained in great detail his notion of positive mental attitude, the creed he'd shared with Koko. Essentially, his strategy was to accept those things that he couldn't do anything about and make the best of the present. Since he had no future, he relied entirely on his fantasies. Actually, it was impressive how well he'd adapted to prison life.

"You know, you're awfully lucky to have this time with me," he reminded again. "There are thousands of people who'd like to be in your place right now."

"I realize that," I said, playing the adoring fan. "I really appreciate all you've done for me." Only a few more minutes and I'd be done with all this groveling.

"Then why are you playing games with me?" he asked. "I have a fine cock. You've seen it. You've seen its mushroom head. You've got to agree it's beautiful."

Since he was looking at me for affirmation, I had no choice but to nod my head.

"Do you know how many guys would love me to shove it up their ass? It's the perfect size."

I was comforted by his relaxed manner. It was as if we were talking sports or something. I don't know if he was feeling sorry for me, or was just more circumspect because there were now more people in the area, but he remained reasonably appropriate throughout the rest of our time together. I suppose he was counting on the next day to follow through on his plan. There was no way I was going to tell him there'd be no next day. In fact, at this point I was thinking his scheduled execution couldn't come too soon.

As the time arrived to say goodbye, he morphed into his charming, personable self, as much for the benefit of Ken and the guards as for me. He seemed convinced that I lacked the power to break away from him. Just to make sure, though, he bestowed on me a few more gifts—another of his paintings, a signed photo of himself for my brother, and a signed copy of his manuscript, *A Question of Doubt*, that was in limited circulation.

"Okay, guys, have a good one," Gacy said as Ken and I walked through the gate.

"See you, John," Ken and I both said in unison. I was so relieved to be leaving Gacy's clutches, I felt giddy. My escape with body—if not full dignity—intact seemed too good to be true. As I was being led out of the prison, I felt for a moment that something was going to happen to me. Perhaps I'd be taken hostage, or Gacy would suddenly decide to attack me from behind with a pen and jab it in my neck. Happily, my premonitions proved false.

I asked Ken to take me back to the motel so I could start packing as soon as possible. Going home was all I could think about.

Later that night, Gacy called to check up on me and that's when I broke the news that I wasn't coming back.

"My dad's in a bad mood," I told him. "I gotta go home. I don't have a choice or he'll beat the shit out of me."

"What do you mean, your father wants you home! Doesn't he know you're supposed to be with me?"

"I know," I said. "He's being ridiculous. But he wants me to come home."

Silence on the other end of the line. I wondered if Gacy had hung up.

"Well," he finally said in frustration, "do you want me to call him to convince him to let you stay?"

Yeah, right, I thought. "No, that'll only make him more upset."

"I can't believe this! I spent all this money to fly you out here—"

I reminded him that it wasn't my fault, that I had no choice in the matter. I was surprised how easily he accepted my explanation. I wondered if he sensed when I left that day that I wouldn't be coming back.

We made plans for a return visit during my summer break. Fat chance of that. Gacy was scheduled to die in a few weeks.

41

Going Home

Okay. I'd made a big mistake. I see that fully now. I began realizing it as I was flying home, trying to fit together the pieces of what had happened to me the previous two days.

It was a midnight flight. I took a window seat so I could stare into the darkness and avoid my fellow passengers. I didn't think I could muster any small talk right now. Besides, I needed to think. In the back of my mind, I wondered whether I knew, the day I set out for Menard, what was going to happen. Had it been a deluded belief in my ability to "handle" people that caused me to ignore the danger signs?

As I listened to the mingled sounds of droning engines and snoring passengers, I seethed. I was furious at Gacy for manipulating me in such a way that I felt bruised, dirty, and vulnerable. I also flagellated myself for not having anticipated Gacy's moves and counteracting them more effectively.

Yes, I'd butted heads with a serial killer and lived to tell about it. I'd climbed into the wolf's cage. But I certainly hadn't tamed him. I may have learned firsthand what it feels like to be so terrified you're frozen in place, but I was going to pay a price. My body may not have been buried beneath Gacy's house, but part of my soul would rest in his trophy case. I was his last victim.

As much as I was hurting, as confused as I felt, the worst part was being so alone. I knew there was nobody I could confide in at home about what had *really* happened. I'd put up a brave front to my parents, minimize the danger I confronted. In fact, I'd tell them very little. And some of what had gone down—well, it was too embarrassing to tell even Jarrod. Gacy's reducing me to tears, for example.

Jarrod had always thought of me as his "cool as a cucumber" older brother—the guy who had everything wired. I needed him to keep believing that. Sometimes it seemed like he was the only member of my fan club.

When I saw my father waiting for me as I exited the plane, I wanted to break into tears and run into his arms. I just wanted him to hold me. But I knew that if I told him what had really happened, the long leash I'd grown accustomed to would be shortened considerably. That would be the end of finding a receptive audience for my next "exciting idea."

"Hi," my father said with a big smile. "How did it go?"

I shrugged. "It was fine. Not what I expected, though."

There it was. The opening. If my father wanted to pick up on that, if he'd decided to press, I probably would have told him. I was that wrung out.

But he didn't.

"So," he said as we made our way past the slot machines to the baggage area, "how was the flight?"

"Fine, Dad." I was both disappointed and relieved that

things would remain private. It was clear to me he didn't really want to know what had happened. In a sense, he was asking for the sanitized version.

He abruptly changed the subject. "Your brother has been difficult to handle lately. Any idea what's been going on with him?"

What *is* this? I wondered. Is he blaming me for Jarrod's problems? I didn't think so. But it made sense that the things I'd been doing were affecting everyone in the household.

The drive home was very quiet and uncharacteristically awkward. I wondered if my father was mad at me but I was afraid to ask. We both were very standoffish, reluctant to get into anything too heavy. Still, I'd missed him terribly and it felt great to be home again. I was even looking forward to returning to school.

I slept most of that day while my parents worked and my brother attended school. I actually barricaded myself in my room, trying to put enough of myself back together to face the world. I brooded about this whole serial killer project I'd embarked on. Despite everything, I still found these individuals fascinating. But Gacy—there was no way I could deal with *him* anymore.

Poor Koko. Now, there was someone I might write. With the bond I'd already established, I figured I could get him to really open up.

Wait a minute! In thinking about him, I realized that what I was engaged in was a form of "self-esteem damage control." It fit a pattern I'd repeated my entire life: experience a setback in one area; make up for it by pushing forward in another area. That way, you avoid failure.

It hadn't occurred to me yet that my visit to Gacy had

258 JASON MOSS

been a success of a certain kind. In fact, by using myself to bait the hook, I'd learned much more about how a predator like him functions than if I'd just sat across from him the whole time and peppered him with questions.

I lay in bed staring at the ceiling, my hands rested on my stomach, fingers intertwined. On an impulse, I moved my right hand to my heart to feel the blood pumping through my body. It felt so good to be alive. Before I drifted off to sleep, my last thought was that I'd do something positive with what I'd learned.

Juggling Killers

So how was Gacy?" my mother asked the next morning. She seemed genuinely concerned about me.

"He was fine," I said nonchalantly, as if we were discussing a relative I'd just visited. "We just talked about his case and what it was like to live in prison."

She nodded, encouraging me to go on. For a change, she seemed interested in what I had to say.

"Nothing else, really," I said, shrugging. "I *did* get to talk to some other people in the prison."

"That must have been interesting."

"Oh, it was. I learned a lot of stuff. I'll tell you this, though. I never want to go to prison. I don't think I could handle it."

"Well, I'm glad everything turned out the way you wanted. Your father and I were very worried about you."

"Yeah, I know." If they had any idea what had really occurred, they'd freak out. "I told you I'd be safe."

She could tell I wasn't revealing everything that had happened. Thankfully, though, instead of prying, she came over and gave me a hug.

"Glad to have you back, Jason."

"Me too, Ma."

I ran upstairs and found Jarrod waiting in my room. He expected a more complete story of what had occurred, so I gave him an edited version, glossing over the more graphic details.

"Hey, I almost forgot," my brother said as he headed out. "You got some mail while you were gone."

I'd asked him to cover for me while I was away and collect any letters that arrived from the other killers I'd been writing. My parents knew I was occasionally corresponding with a few inmates, but they had no idea of the extent of my involvement, or how often my pen pals checked in.

I'd been away only three days but there were letters from both Charles Manson and Richard Ramirez waiting. I couldn't even begin to concentrate on them. I was still reeling from all that had happened in Illinois. I just wanted to take a shower for about a week, to wash away the embarrassment that was still clinging to me.

I decided not to open the letters yet. I wanted to clear my mind and focus on more pleasant things. I was looking forward to spending time with Jenn, getting together with some of my friends, just hanging out with my family.

In spite of my resolve to chill out, though, Gacy redoubled his assault on my life. He called me that very night.

"So, buddy," he said cheerfully, "how was the trip back?"

"Fine," I answered. It was hard to hide my fury. In fact, I was kicking myself for having answered the phone.

"Your family okay?" he prodded further when the silence went on for endless seconds.

"Yeah, no problems. Everything's cool."

"Well, then, I'd better let you get back to things. Just wanted to see how you're doing. Make sure you got back okay."

The conversation ended awkwardly. I hoped that maybe he'd gotten the message to fade away. That wasn't to be, though.

I was still trying to determine what I wanted to do about Ramirez and Manson, whether I wanted to keep those relationships going, when two letters arrived from Gacy the next day. Then another letter the following day.

In each of them, he expressed his disappointment and anger that I'd left a day early. He said he was hoping that I'd consider moving to Chester, Illinois, so I could be near him and visit him every day. He said he was sure Ken could find a house there for me to stay at.

I couldn't believe how deluded he was. He seemed oblivious to the revulsion I'd shown at the prison. He'd superimposed this fantasy on me, and when he thought of me, he couldn't keep the two separate. Though it was possible I might learn additional things about him—and thus, about serial killers in general—by continuing a desultory relationship with him, I'd lost the stomach for it. I just wanted him to go away.

As more letters from him arrived, I left them unopened and unanswered. I hooked up an answering machine with caller ID so I could avoid his calls. I hoped he'd finally get the message.

Meanwhile, I decided to break off things with Ramirez and Manson as well, at least for a while. That left only two other killer pen pals—Henry Lee Lucas and Elmer Wayne Henley. I'd written them before I left for Illinois.

Lucas was particularly interesting. Years before, he'd

been arrested for illegal possession of a firearm, and while in custody confessed to over three hundred murders. Beginning at age fourteen, when he raped and killed a girl his own age, and extending until he was twenty-three, when he killed his own mother, he took lives indiscriminately. He was imprisoned for murdering his mom, but was subsequently paroled. Free again, he killed many others, most of them anonymous hitchhikers.

I knew that Lucas, like Gacy, fancied himself an artist, so I approached him by posing as an art dealer who might be interested in selling his work. Though he wrote me several times, most of his letters centered around his desperate need for money. I never seemed to get beyond business with him, so eventually I let the relationship wither away.

Elmer Wayne Henley was only seventeen when he joined a gang of serial killers who abducted twenty-seven young boys, raped them repeatedly, tortured them, and then killed them. Some of the victims were as young as nine years old. I read that they'd even preyed on two brothers, which I found especially disturbing.

Given Henley's youth and naiveté, I thought a direct approach might work. Certainly, if it succeeded, it would be easier on me than trying to play several different characters at once. I just told him about myself, and said I wanted to be his friend. I sent along a photo and an open invitation to respond. I almost forgot about him because nearly two months elapsed before I received a return letter.

He was most apologetic, even pitifully so, for not having written earlier. He talked about wanting to write me on a regular basis, but there was something about the intimacy he imagined with me that frightened him.

"[I have] a tendency to withdraw," he wrote. "For a good

proportion of my time I was in contact only with my family and no others."

He explained that he'd taught himself to do time in prison by isolating himself as much as possible. "I'm good at that," he said. There was something about my letter to him, though, that he couldn't ignore—something that drew him out of his shell.

I was skeptical that he'd follow through on his promise to write on a regular basis. After I wrote him again and received a very superficial response, I abandoned the relationship.

Since Gacy continued to make efforts to contact me, I decided that rather than confront him directly and suffer whatever wrath he might be capable of, I would ease gently out of the relationship. After the prison visit, I no longer underestimated him. I'd concluded he was capable of reaching out from prison and, while maybe not physically harming me, certainly making trouble.

So in a letter I wrote to him, I dropped hints that my father's behavior was increasingly violent and erratic. I said my dad was enraged by all the collect calls I'd accepted, hundreds of dollars each month. I told Gacy that my father had spent the reimbursement checks on booze, so when it came time to pay the bills, there was no money left. What I was trying to do was send the message that, very shortly, access to me was going to be denied.

Since Gacy might very likely drag out the heavy artillery to get me to fix the situation, no matter what remedy was called for, or, alternatively, fire off a few smear salvos out of sheer vengeance, I decided it was time to confess all to my parents. As much as I dreaded owning up to my bad judgment, I needed to protect myself in case Gacy deployed his weapons, as illusory as some of them were.

"Well," I began hesitantly, addressing my family in the living room. "Uh . . ." When I stammered like this, they knew I was going to hit them with something big, either one of my crazy ideas or a mea culpa of impressive magnitude.

Dad nodded his head in encouragement. Mom shook her head, as if to say, *Oh God, what now!*

I revealed everything that had occurred during the previous months. I specified the number of people I'd been writing to and the volume of mail I'd received. I went into considerable detail regarding Gacy, explaining that I'd created two sets of letters to entice his interest. I also admitted that I was worried he might try to use the fictitious content of the letters to smear me—and by extension, them.

Mercifully, the family meeting went far better than I imagined. We agreed it would be useful to get some legal help in constructing an affidavit which stated that the incidents described in the letters were fictitious. As it turned out, my mother refused to sign the affidavit. She said she wanted me to learn that I couldn't always rely on *her* to get myself out of trouble.

Well, I suppose she could have refused to talk to me for the rest of my natural life. All in all, the upshot of my full disclosure seemed remarkably painless.

It really seemed like my long nightmare was finally coming to an end. At least, the waking part. I figured I nearly had Gacy back in his Pandora's box, so to speak. I thought I'd confronted, and dealt with, all the aspects of his personality.

I was grossly mistaken.

43

Blackmail

"Jason, this is Ken, I'm on a conference call, I'll talk to you later . . . Bye."

"Hello. Hello. John, are you there?" I heard Ken say again, making sure Gacy was still on the line.

"Yeah, hello," Gacy replied. "Was he there?"

"No, I got the recording."

I'd just run up to my room when I heard the phone ringing. The answering machine picked up on the fourth ring. Apparently, there was something wrong with the machine because it kept recording the conversation between Ken and Gacy, who thought they were disconnected from my line.

Throughout the previous week, I'd been able to avoid most of Gacy's calls. Using caller ID and the answering machine, I'd set up a pretty effective screen. Gacy's current ploy, however, was to have Ken call me and try to conference him in.

Due to a technical glitch, my machine was continuing to broadcast this conversation, which focused mostly on legal aspects of Gacy's latest appeal. And since I'd set the machine on "unlimited," it was recording everything.

I sat on the bed amused as I listened in. They were arguing. Ken was upset that Gacy had never given him a copy of the privately published book Gacy had given me when I left.

"Why don't you ask Jason to make you a copy?" Gacy said, laughing.

"Because . . . because I didn't . . . I don't feel comfortable asking him." Ken seemed jealous of the attention Gacy had shown me.

"In any case, if we don't get back to him . . ."

The next part of the conversation was unintelligible, maybe because Gacy was mumbling to himself rather than actually talking.

". . . Jason has not come through with what he said, which means he's violated . . . I don't have to observe his trust anymore as long as he's gonna lie to me."

"What are we looking for?" Ken asked. "The notice, the confidentiality agreement, and copies of the pictures?"

They were referring to a number of legal documents Gacy routinely asked his visitors to sign. The documents, which had been drawn up by his attorneys, were his insurance that a visitor wouldn't repeat any confessions Gacy inadvertently made.

Several times prior to my going to the prison, Gacy had tried to get me to sign the documents, but I always stalled him with excuses. Now he was asking Ken to find my signed papers so he could ensure my silence. That was going to be difficult because no such papers existed. Gacy had by now learned from Ken, and also from Koko, that I hadn't matched up with the person he'd described to them.

Now he was not only suspicious regarding what game I might be playing, he was furious that I was refusing to speak with him.

He kept ranting about getting even. "I'll send those letters [the ones that detailed my fictitious incestuous forays] to his father," he threatened.

As I watched the little tape in the machine going round and round, I thanked the instincts that had told me a few days before to go to my parents and tell them what I'd been up to.

"I don't like people playing games with me," Gacy continued.

"Hey, believe me, I know that!" said Ken. I knew Ken well enough by now to believe he wished me no ill will; he was just trying to keep Gacy's gaskets from blowing.

"I've been more than fair and generous with him, and to play this holdout game with the phone . . . Come on . . . I have never held out on the phone. Tell me when I even didn't make the phone bill good?"

"Yeah, John, you're right."

"He's had more than enough money to cover the phone bill. I've given him over $475 for the phone."

"Yeah, I know," Ken said, desperately trying to appease him. "I'll have to find out what's going on."

"You ask him if he'd like it if I turned his letters over to the Las Vegas police. See if he likes that. Make it a point that he should know not to piss me off."

I couldn't believe that this whole blackmail plan was being recorded. What were the odds? I kept expecting the machine to click off at any time. But it didn't. It just kept recording and recording.

The conversation had moved back to one of the appeals when Gacy abruptly changed the subject.

"I still think Jason is playing games with me. 'Cause I did nothing wrong to him, and here it's been a month I've been denied talking to him."

"Yeah."

"I still miss all the goddamn letters he was sending me. And none of his letters has been written as loose as they were written before. It's like he's on guard."

"Yeah . . . well . . . maybe he's afraid."

Ken's remark seemed to ignite something in Gacy, because his voice rattled the answering machine speaker: "Yeah, well, I got news for you, *never* play both ends against the middle with me, because it will backfire."

"I know," Ken said, forcing laughter. "I would never even think of that." More strained laughter followed.

"Well . . . he'll go down harder than a rock. Same thing with his brother, not answering my letters. 'Cause if he thinks I'm kidding, I'm not. And once the ball gets rolling, there'll be no stopping it."

He then began describing how he was going to contact an old friend in Las Vegas from the time when he lived here. I wasn't sure whether he was planning to pay him to hurt me, but I'd had enough. The sight of the incriminating tape sitting there in my machine gave me the confidence to finally stand up to this monster, to reveal the *real* Jason.

I picked up the phone and said, "Hello, John."

Complete silence on the other end.

"Oh," Gacy said softly, "where were you when we called before?"

"I was still at school." Gosh, I was enjoying this. "I want

to talk to you about this call. Ken never clicked over and my machine recorded the whole thing."

"What do you mean?" Gacy asked, knowing exactly what I meant.

"You know what I mean. I have it all here on my machine, how you're going to send the letters to the police. Go right ahead. I have your whole conversation with Ken on tape."

The other end of the line was completely still. For a moment, I wondered if they'd hung up, but then I heard Gacy's characteristic mouth-breathing.

"Feel free, John, to tell the police. Everyone here knows that I was just studying you for school. I let everyone know about the content of the letters before I'd even written them. The police already have a copy of them just in case you tried any bullshit like this."

Okay, I was stretching things. But I wanted to make sure he knew that any leverage he thought he had had just slipped through his fingers. I wanted nothing to do with him anymore.

To underscore *my* leverage, I said, "I bet *Hard Copy* or *Inside Edition* would be very interested in hearing about how John Wayne Gacy tried to blackmail two children, how he tried to get them to have sex together just for his amusement. Don't forget, I've got the whole damn thing on tape."

"You think so, huh?"

There was no bluster in Gacy's voice. He sounded tired. Defeated.

Then I heard a click on the phone and the tape stopped circling. That was the last time I spoke to John Wayne Gacy.

11

Execution

It wasn't easy putting back together the pieces of my life. I'd been neglecting my relationship with Jenn and with my friends. Things were still tense at home, especially after Gacy's threats of blackmail. My schoolwork had suffered— for the first time in my life, I wasn't doing my assignments early. How I'd managed to get As while being caught up in all this still amazes me.

I felt somewhat depressed as well, because although I was glad to be rid of Gacy and my other pen pals, I'd enjoyed the excitement. Without their bizarre behavior to examine, my life now seemed fairly boring.

Still, there were compensations: the time away from Jenn seemed to make us both more giving and appreciative. And Jarrod was ecstatic that he had his brother back—that I wasn't as distracted as I'd been the previous months.

There was, however, one last piece of unfinished business: Gacy was due to be put to death and I wasn't sure how I felt about that.

I still feared him. I continued to have trouble sleeping. At times I hated him more than I've ever hated anyone. I prayed to God that this time he'd finally be executed. Seven times in the past it had been postponed, and there was no reason to believe it wouldn't happen again. I knew for sure that Gacy thought he still had a few more tricks up his sleeve.

The media attention surrounding the scheduled execution was enormous. I couldn't turn on the television or open a newspaper without seeing Gacy's smiling face. And each time I glimpsed it, the memories would come flooding back—of his standing over me, wagging his penis in my face, and me sobbing helplessly. No matter what else I lived through, that image would forever be burned into my brain.

If there was an upside to all this, it was that I was now a celebrity among my friends. A feature article had appeared in the local newspaper about my visiting Gacy for a school project, and when I walked around campus, people I hardly knew would call out, "So they're gonna smoke your friend, huh?"

Actually, there'd be no smoke involved, since lethal injection was the preferred method of execution in Illinois. I told myself that I couldn't wait for the needle to be inserted, that once the deadly liquid ran into his veins he'd be out of my life forever.

The part I kept buried at the time is that I could never have administered the lethal dose myself. No matter how much I feared and hated him, I couldn't wish what was going to happen to him on anyone. I imagined him in his cell with all his bravado, all his charm, pretending to the world that he was fearless. I knew how terrified he really was.

This might sound ridiculous, but I began wondering if Gacy had a soul. I wondered if someone who was that evil, who'd destroyed so many lives, who was so willing to be deceptive and manipulative, could possibly have anything resembling a spiritual side to him. If so, I wondered if he'd haunt me from the grave.

The day of the execution, Jenn joined my family as we sat around the television waiting for the latest report. The media had been calling me for comments because I was a local connection to a story that, by now, had spilled beyond America's borders and gone international. While I answered reporters' questions, bantered with Jenn and my brother, sparred with my mother, and talked with my dad, I kept thinking about Gacy. I felt really sad. I thought about how alone and scared he was probably feeling.

Except for my grandfather, who'd died when I was young, Gacy was the first person I'd known whose life was about to be snuffed out. As the spectacle unfolded on television, there were shots of protesters outside the prison . . . interviews with relatives of the victims . . . footage showing where the execution would take place, the gurney he'd lie down on, and the straps that would hold him in place. The camera lingered on the IV tubes that would deliver first a double dose of sodium pentothal to sedate him and then a combination of pancuronium bromide to stop his breathing and potassium chloride to stop his heart. The executioners seemed to have thought of everything.

Normally, this is supposed to be a simple, quick, and relatively painless procedure, but in Gacy's case, there was a glitch.

"Ladies and gentlemen," the news announcer said, "I'm being told there's some type of delay. They've closed the curtain in the execution chamber. I don't have much information right now, but it seems there's been some type of problem with the administration of the chemicals. This is all I know at this point in time. I'll keep you posted as soon as further information becomes available."

Everyone in my house sat motionless, waiting for a report that would clear up what was going on. "Hey, Jason," my brother teased, "looks like he escaped again." Chuckles filled the room—a few contributed by me, though I had to force them out. Actually, I'd been apprehensive that something like this would happen, that somehow I'd have to live with the prospect that Gacy would keep pestering and threatening me. I'd imagined the Supreme Court intervening. Or possibly the governor. But I'd never dreamed Gacy would be rescued by a faulty catheter.

While Jenn and my family chattered away, eating pizza and chicken fingers my mother had ordered, I silently prayed, *Please, God, let this nightmare be over. Let Gacy finally die.*

It took eighteen minutes before Gacy finally stopped breathing and was pronounced dead, double the time that had been allotted. When they made the announcement, my mother and brother cheered. *"Yessss!"* they whooped, fists held above their outstretched arms.

Jarrod gave me a high five, then Jenn reached over and hugged me, whispering in my ear, "The monster is dead."

After a few minutes of idle chatter, I politely excused myself and went up to my room to be alone. I looked through some of the letters Gacy had sent me, especially those in which he'd been rather normal and almost considerate. I stared at his paintings, haunting images that revealed so transparently how tortured he'd been. Then I put them all in the safe, and when I locked the door, I hoped I was putting this chapter in my life behind me.

A few days later, Ken called to pass along a last message that Gacy had left for me. I shuddered, wondering if I really wanted to hear it or not.

Before I could decide, he said, "On the last day of his life, the day he was executed, he asked about you, Jason. He wanted to know if I'd kept in contact with you. He asked how you were doing. I told him I'd last talked to you about a week or so before, and that you were doing all right and that you were just finishing up with school and your finals.

"Like I once told you," he continued, "I think he genuinely cared about you, Jason. At least the only way he could. He certainly ended up respecting you. He knew he'd met his match with you. He kept saying you really took him for a ride. He'd say it in anger but I think he got a kick out of it, too."

Tears started falling down my face as I heard those words. It sort of reminded me of those Westerns in which the two adversaries grudgingly show respect for each other, just before they reach for their guns. For a long time, that had been the fantasy I'd been living out—that I was a gunslinger wearing a white hat taking on the cold-blooded killer wearing the black hat.

I'd learned, though, that life isn't a movie. Though it's nice to believe in white-hatted heroes and black-hatted villains, people are a lot more complex than that. Myself—I figured my Stetson had a few stains on it. And Gacy— well, you had to look awfully hard to find a speck of white on his black fedora. But I liked to think that everybody had a little good in them somewhere. Maybe, in Gacy's case, it was there as a child—before abuse took his innocence away.

45

Aftermath

"Yeah, *right*."

"No way!"

"That really happened, Jason?"

I wasn't surprised by their challenges. I was used to it by now. In fact, I was downright amused by their expressions—grins of half-disbelief, half-amazement.

I was standing in front of a psychology class at the high school I'd graduated from, the school Jarrod now attended. I'd been invited to tell my story, the one that had been splashed across the local papers and had now become the stuff of legend in Las Vegas: "Boy takes on serial killers. Actually makes friends with them. Even visits them in prison."

It had been two years since I'd escaped Gacy's clutches, and a year since I'd ceased virtually all communication with serial killers. Though my presence in this classroom today might have belied it, I was trying to move past that phase of my life. I was now enjoying working with the victims of misfortune rather than the perpetrators of violence.

For a while, I'd been living with a burn victim as an

aide. Not only did she have to contend with chronic pain from third-degree burns that covered most of her body, but she'd also been diagnosed with the AIDS virus.

I was also a "Wish Grantor" for the local chapter of the Make-a-Wish Foundation. That involved spending time interviewing terminally ill children to discover what they wanted as their most prized fantasy. For one child, I helped arrange a meeting with the Air Force Thunderbirds; for others, it might be a dog to keep them company or a trip to Disneyland. Giving comfort to dying children helped push away the dark clouds that sometimes settled over me.

I'd volunteered to be a Big Brother as well. I was assigned to mentor an eleven-year-old boy whose father had left him and his family when he was just five. I felt privileged to be the friend, confidant, and teacher the boy so desperately needed.

All of these activities, besides being satisfying ways to make a difference, were an attempt on my part to learn more about what victims felt. After all, I'd been a victim myself. If I was ever to become a prosecutor, or a forensic psychologist, or a federal agent—my career ambitions fluctuated daily—I'd need to see things from the victim's side.

I suppose, too, that a couple other motives entered into it. I'd always enjoyed being in control. It feels so powerful to be able to grant a wish to a dying child, to mentor a fatherless boy, or to make a difference in the lives of those who need help the most. Too, I probably felt safer around people who wouldn't try to hurt me. As a result of seeing firsthand the evil that people are capable of, I was still grappling with some trust issues.

I'm not sure why I'd consented to speak to this group of high schoolers at a time when I was trying to leave the past behind. I guess, partly, it was a favor to my old teacher; and, partly, a way to help Jarrod with his audacity-loving peer group. He'd get some mileage out of my talk when they convened for their next bullshit session.

As much as I appreciated the attention of the twenty-eight students, a part of me was wishing I could get through my remarks as soon as possible and get back to my real life—the one in which I was now known as president of UNLV's Psychology Honors Society and chief justice of the student council. The days of staying closeted in my room, playing the recluse, were past.

"So, Jason," one eager, not unattractive girl asked me, "what made you do such a crazy thing [visit the prison] in the first place? I mean, did you really think you'd be safe?"

I'd been asked the same questions so many times over the last two years, there was a tendency to go on autopilot. I tried to think of new ways of explaining myself, new images that would make it all clear.

"It's complicated really," I stumbled. "It's more like—"

"Did you see anyone electrocuted while you were there?" a boy interrupted. I could see eyes roll, as if off-the-wall questions were this kid's stock-in-trade. He looked barely awake. Throughout the first half hour of my talk, he'd been resting his head on his arms, either drugged out or exhausted from lack of sleep. Before I could even reply, his head dropped back into his arms.

Miss Lawrence jumped in to redirect the discussion back to the subject she was hoping we'd explore more. "Jason," she asked, "what did you learn from all of this? I mean, you've been through so much. You did things that most people wouldn't even dream of. I know I wouldn't."

The class laughed at that—but not because they thought

it was true. Miss Lawrence had a reputation for being a fearless risk-taker herself. I think they were laughing because they knew she'd love to try something equally audacious.

I found myself hesitating, thinking desperately of how to reply.

"Yo, Jay-*son*," a wiseass in the front row called out, seeing I was struggling with my answer.

The problem was I couldn't tell these kids what I'd *really* learned. The actual story would be too upsetting. And, frankly, I didn't have the courage. These kids—the ones not wisecracking or sleeping, at least—saw me as some kind of hero. I couldn't tell them about my regrets, about the damage I'd done to my family, about the ways I'd hurt my brother, about the misery I'd known. I couldn't describe the clashes with my mother, or how much conflict had been involved in getting my parents to go along with my plans. I couldn't tell them how sorry I was about the pain I'd caused.

"Well," I said finally, trying to come up with a lesson the kids could take away, "I learned that when you do some tough things, when you put yourself out there, it opens doors for you in the future."

"Like what?" the guy in the front row challenged.

"Like . . . getting to work for the United States Secret Service."

"No way!"

"Way," I replied, starting to like this boy now. Whereas the other kids seemed compliant and passive, this guy really seemed inquisitive. I recognized a part of me in him.

"Actually, I did an internship with the Secret Service office here in Las Vegas. I even got to meet the president and his wife when they were in town for a campaign stop."

I could hear snickering from the back of the room. Now I knew what teachers went through; they missed all the best stuff. I was curious to know what the kids were whispering about.

"You," I pointed to one of the girls in the back of the room who'd been talking. "Did you have a question you want to ask?"

She just giggled and whispered something to her friend again. Then she looked up and smiled.

I stood in front of the room, rocking back and forth on my feet, deciding where to go next. I looked up at the clock and saw we still had a few minutes left. I took a deep breath and decided to say out loud what I'd been thinking.

"Look, I know this story sounds interesting and all. But it wasn't really like that. I mean, I'm not the same anymore, the same person I used to be. After writing and talking to guys like Manson and Ramirez and Gacy, knowing the ways they really think, I can't get it out of my head that there are still so many others like them around."

Most of the kids now showed that kind of engrossed look you see when you're telling a ghost story. They were a little on edge but they couldn't wait for me to continue.

"I'm pretty mistrustful of people I come into contact with. I question everyone's motives. I wonder what they really want from me, and how they're going to manipulate me to get it."

I paused for a moment and scanned the room to see if they were following. I noticed the guy in front was definitely relating to what I was saying.

"I still have nightmares that Gacy and other killers are

out there trying to hunt and kill me. Sometimes, when I'm alone in my car or in my room, when I'm drifting off to sleep, I feel the touch of Ramirez's huge hand or I hear the rhythm of Manson's poetry. Often I see the inside of Gacy's cell—remember what it smelled like. I wish I could get these things out of my head, but I can't."

"How else are you different, Jason?" Miss Lawrence asked. Bless her heart. She was trying to get me to focus on a more positive part of the experience.

I glanced at the clock again, hoping to be saved by the bell. Alas, still a few interminable minutes left.

"Well, for one thing, now I'm more focused on school. When I was here at Green Valley High School, I was a good student. Better than good. The only B I ever got in my life was that first semester at UNLV when all these events were taking place. Ever since then, I've buckled down even more. The things I want to do in life are going to take everything I have to get there."

I could see Miss Lawrence beaming in the back of the room. This is the message every teacher loves to hear from an ex-student: study hard, work hard, and the world will open up to you.

But that wasn't where I was headed.

"Look, I wouldn't wish the way I am on anyone." I raised my voice louder, hoping to wake up the two guys with their heads down in the back of the room. "I wish I didn't know about all the dangers out there. I wish I didn't know so much about how killers and psychopaths think. I wish I could just enjoy being in college like my friends do. Party-hearty."

There was a smattering of laughter around the room. When the two sleepers raised their heads, I figured I'd scored a major breakthrough. Either that or they sensed the bell was about to ring.

Now I was racing against the clock, trying to get out everything I was thinking. I'm pretty sure Miss Lawrence understood me. Maybe even a few of the kids, too.

I realized how much more I valued life. I remembered being in eleventh grade like these kids, thinking I was immortal. Death was a word that had no meaning for me. That wasn't true anymore. Now I knew death intimately.

The bell rang. Most of the kids scrambled out the door without a look in my direction. I couldn't blame them really. The school was so big it took every one of the ten minutes to get to their next class on time. But a few of the kids solemnly made their way to the front of the room to shake my hand or thank me for coming. Miss Lawrence, too, was effusive in her gratitude: she knew how much I'd revealed that day.

I walked out through the open courtyard, reminiscing about the four years of my life I'd spent in this school as a member of its first graduating class. I passed the corridor where I used to see Jenn standing by her locker . . . the lunchroom where I hung out with my friends . . . and the weight room where I thought I was supplying myself with as much strength as I needed for the future. It was a time of innocence for me, a time before I faced monsters.

The hot, sauna winds of April blew sand in my face once I emerged from the school's courtyard into the parking lot. Automatically, I began to head toward where my reserved parking space had once been. Realizing my mistake, I smiled and turned back toward the guest spaces in front.

It was time to head home. Mom was making our favorite dinner tonight, spaghetti with meat sauce. I vowed to make an extra effort to be nice to her. I realized now what I'd put her through all these years, what I'd put everyone through. I probably couldn't change my inquisitive nature, but I intended to make it up to them somehow. If I could just learn from the pain I'd gone through, if only others could learn as well, then maybe it all would have been worth it.

For now, though, most nights before I go to sleep, before I even turn out the light and climb into bed, I hesitate for a moment. There've been too many nights during which I awaken suddenly, absolutely convinced Gacy, Dahmer, Manson, Lucas, or Ramirez is standing in my room, watching me sleep. I can see their eyes glowing in the dark—hear their heavy, ragged breathing.

Sometimes I can even hear Gacy taunt me: "Jason . . . Jason . . . wake up and come with me. You can't hide from me now . . . You won't escape again." Then suddenly a pair of blood-soaked hands reach down for my throat, squeezing so hard that I gasp for breath and wake myself up in a cold sweat.

Gacy was certainly right. I haven't been able to escape him after all. During the days I keep myself as busy as I can. I distract myself with my various projects. I volunteer my time helping others.

It's at night that there's no place to hide.

Afterword
by Jeffrey Kottler,
Ph.D.

Even though Jason elected to break off all contact with his "pen pals" for a time after Gacy's execution, he still remained active refining his methods of interrogation and questioning. Through the next four years of college, he learned everything he could about the psychology of criminal behavior. He built a personal library that included the most scholarly works in the field. He volunteered to do research with his psychology professors. He studied hard during his internships with the Secret Service and Bureau of Alcohol, Tobacco, and Firearms. And the writing of this book seemed to rekindle in him the desire to resume his own research efforts, to prepare himself for a career in law enforcement and forensic psychology.

Which is why a few months after our collaboration on this project ended, I found myself by Jason's side in the waiting room of Death Row in a Huntsville, Texas, prison. We were there to interview Henry Lee Lucas, who was soon to be scheduled for execution (the sentence was subsequently commuted by the governor because of prosecutorial bungling during his trial). I was curious to see Jason in action, going toe to toe with Lucas. Would he seem out of his depth, as he had with Gacy? I wondered how much he'd learned since his first traumatic encounter.

Things did not go well at first. Although Lucas, Jason, and I were the only ones in the huge, cavernous visiting area, our subject was behaving as if there were eavesdroppers. Perhaps there were.

I could see from the corner of my eye that Jason was becoming as frustrated as I was. Lucas was just so evasive, with his smug smile. Jason and I had been playing tag team, each of us directing various questions his way, rarely sure of who was leading whom.

I was about ready to pack it in. We were mostly wasting our time, and I felt uncomfortable spending even a minute with this squirrely guy who'd stabbed his own mother to death, as well as bludgeoned and strangled dozens of others. I was about to give Jason the "we're outta here" signal when he pressed his foot against mine and looked at me intently. He'd obviously devised some sort of plan, and he wanted me to play along.

"Henry," he began, using a different tone of voice to indicate a change in subject, "we were wondering if you could help us with a project we're working on."

"Sure. If I can. Whatcha got in mind?" At that moment I imagined that if his hands hadn't been cuffed, they'd surely be rubbing each other with glee. *Maybe there's some angle I can exploit*, you could hear him thinking.

"We're working on a movie script," Jason continued, "and we could use some input. It's sort of like you'd be our consultant."

Lucas didn't say a word at first. You could see his

wheels turning, see him calculating the chances of getting some money out of this to finance his various legal appeals.

"What's it about?" he asked.

"Just down your line," Jason said without a beat. "It's about a killer."

They both smiled at one another, as if they had an understanding. Lucas nodded but remained silent. Waiting. Watching.

"See," Jason said, "we've got this character who kills people, but we need to know a lot more about what's involved. We figured that with all your personal research and all, you must know some things that could help make this movie realistic."

I couldn't believe how quickly the flow of the conversation changed once Jason had created this vehicle for Lucas to speak more honestly. While Lucas had previously been reticent and terse, answering in monosyllables, all of a sudden he talked as if he was delivering a seminal lecture on his area of expertise (which of course he was).

"If you don't leave evidence," Lucas said conspiratorially, "they can't find you."

"Uh huh," Jason responded, waiting for him to continue.

"If you don't tell nobody, you won't get caught neither." Lucas's big mistake had been to work with a partner.

"You have to hide the body so it won't be found. It's good to burn a body, but then they still find teeth, so you have to hide it real good."

I looked over at Jason as this conversation ensued. Although I interview people for a living, I was grudgingly impressed by the skill and artistry with which he guided the discussion.

"Choppin' up a body makes a mess and it leaves evidence," Lucas explained. "You don't want to have blood."

At this Jason and I simply nodded our heads, as if Lucas was passing along a cherished family recipe.

"Everyone urinates. You take the average guy, he messes himself. But a younger girl, they just urinate. The older ones, they do both."

I couldn't believe the conversation's direction. Slowly, Lucas had forgotten that he was talking about killing in general and had segued into his own experiences. At least it appeared that way.

"So, how do you find victims?" Jason bore in, dropping the pretense about consulting for a movie.

"That's easy. You can find people anywhere—motels, clubs, parking lots, grocery stores. If you like kids, you can go to schools or find them on the streets. You can drive anywhere, see what you want, and just get it. But you gotta have the nerve. If you don't have the nerve, don't bother."

"Makes sense," Jason deadpanned.

"Yeah, you got to get people away from others 'cause they scream a lot. You make short cuts," said Lucas, showing us in pantomime how to torture a victim with a knife. "You kind of design 'em, is what you call it."

Jason and I both nodded our heads. I was dumbfounded. Couldn't say a word if I'd wanted to.

"Never commit a murder the same way," Lucas continued, "that is, if you want to get away with it." He seemed to be checking things off in his head. And all the while I couldn't stifle the thought that these rules he was listing matched exactly the methodology he had used to commit his own crimes.

"You need to travel a lot, always switch cars, do it different each time, a different way."

Yes, this is *exactly* what he did.

"Do your stuff at night," he instructed, his one good eye (the other is glass) looking off into the distance as if he was fondly recalling favorite murders. Then his eye locked back on us, and his characteristically soft voice became firm: "You gotta pick someone up at night."

He continued, checking off another dozen items that any self-respecting serial killer should take into consideration when practicing his craft. Finally, he got to the last on his list.

"Most of all"—he laughed briefly, then coughed into his hand—"don't confess." Then he started laughing again.

As amazed as I was by Lucas's frankness, I was more impressed by the skill Jason had shown in procuring this information.

Even now, I look at him and can't believe how young he is.

In the end, what are we to make of Jason's story?

Even before publication, this account has found sufficient readers to make it possible to categorize the most common reactions. They are:

(1) "Jason is probably a budding sociopath and serial killer himself—he did this research so he wouldn't make the same mistakes as those who got caught."

(2) "Jason is some kind of weirdo who's confused about his sexual identity and who used his correspondence to try out different roles."

(3) "Jason was a self-centered kid whose youth pre-

vented him from appreciating how dangerous and misguided his actions were."

(4) "Jason is a complex, nervy risk-taker driven at times
by noble objectives and at other times by motives deeply
rooted in his unusual upbringing."

It is the last category of opinion that I think comes clos-
est to the truth. I can assure you that Jason is hardly a budding criminal, nor is he sexually confused. True, he can
come across as self-important, but remember, these were
the actions of an eighteen-year-old boy trying to prove himself. He was attempting to escape conflicts at home, yet
afraid to venture too far away. He wanted to distinguish
himself in some way but felt he could only do so by competing with others. Such was the emptiness of his egoistic
pursuits that he continually found himself taking on more
grandiose projects, hoping for the triumph that would bol-
ster his esteem and prove to others he was special.

Like most of us, Jason has a dark side, a part of himself
that is both repulsed by and drawn to violence and murder.
The difference is that rather than merely read books or see
movies about killers, he wants to get still closer to these
predators, perhaps even to slay them symbolically. There is
certainly an altruistic motive to Jason's behavior; he really
does enjoy the role of white knight rescuing the peasants
from marauding bandits. His college years were devoted to
one social service job after another, and I predict that will
continue well into his adult life.

Jason would, however, be the first to admit that he genuinely enjoys stepping into the deviant world, especially
among those who obey no rules except those they create.
Does he want to be like these killers? Again, I don't think

so. I believe him when he says that he wants to conquer, or at least understand, that which terrifies him the most. I also think that, like many of us, he is intrigued with the novelty and intense visceral stimulation that comes from studying the behavior of chronic killers. These are people who engage in the most ruthless behavior imaginable without a hint of remorse. They laugh in the face of danger—at least the kind they can control.

Jason's narrative brings up several aspects that warrant further exploration. The first can be summed up by a remark I've often heard from people who've read the story: "How did he ever get his parents to let him do such a thing?" Indeed, it *is* hard to believe that anyone would let their kid spend his spring break on Death Row, alone in a cell with a killer.

In this lone respect, I think Jason's narrative fails to do justice to his guile. In my judgment, Jason's parents are honest, hardworking, responsible people. They care deeply about the welfare of their sons and have devoted their lives to giving them the best shot at life possible. In spite of their complaints about how difficult Jason was to raise, they're immensely proud of what he has accomplished.

In reflecting on their allowing Jason to pursue his project to such bizarre lengths, I chalk it up to his infuriating effectiveness as a persuader. If Jason decided that he wanted to do something, I don't believe anyone could stop him, least of all his parents, who had other problems to deal with.

A second aspect of the story that merits further comment is its portrayal of the "point of transaction" between killer and victim—the exact moment when the prey is reeled in.

Prior to Jason's account, we actually knew very little about this encounter and why otherwise intelligent, capable individuals wound up being deceived and trapped.

I find it significant that Jason, a kickboxer and weightlifter who towered over Gacy, was brought under the killer's complete control by words alone. In spite of Jason's rationalizations that he could have overpowered Gacy at any moment, it appears that he was saved by the bell—or, rather, was rescued by Gacy's nephew, who happened to arrive on the scene. Even today this nags at Jason—it was okay to *pretend* to be a victim, but he'll never forgive himself for actually being trapped in that role.

Credit Gacy, who was as sensitive and perceptive as any trained psychologist, for sizing up Jason's vulnerabilities (just as Jason was doing with Gacy). By alternating between two distinct personas—by switching from good cop to bad cop—he was able to keep the young man off balance.

Of course, victims like Jason are not only paralyzed by the killer himself but by the very *idea* of him. Throughout his prison visit, the thought repeatedly passed through Jason's mind, "I can't believe who this guy is! I can't believe what he's done! To think these same hands touching me now also killed dozens of others." This sort of thinking can turn even the strongest legs to jelly.

Where Jason erred most was in his own perceived invincibility. Like any young person, and certainly like any amateur, he believed himself infallible. He made the one mistake that a police officer learns the first day on the job: don't underestimate anyone. Jason certainly possessed a seasoned cop's suspicious nature, but he lacked the experience. He got carried away with himself, lost his objectivity, turned the whole episode into a test of his virility. It was as if he was big-game hunting, after the most dangerous animal he could imagine; no matter what happened, he intended to win in the end. If he hadn't caught Gacy on tape confessing to blackmail, I'm convinced he would have found another way to feel like he'd captured his prize.

The same was true with the others as well. Jason believed he could outwit, out-think, and outmaneuver any of the killers. Perhaps so, provided the competition was locked in cages. One can appreciate, though, that once these guys are on the outside (and there are *hundreds* of them currently on the loose), targeted victims have little chance to escape their clutches.

Ultimately, Jason's adventure leaves us with a number of insights. For example, Jason discovered a whole world of deception operating within the network of Death Rows across the nation. Several of the killers confessed to massive fabrications during their debriefings by police and psychologists. In these sessions, they admitted to crimes they never committed. They used information they'd gained from other inmates to muddle investigations in progress and they learned to fudge their responses on supposedly sophisticated psychological instruments. Authorities forget that just as they themselves share data and consult with one another, so too do various killers.

Jason's account also warns of the extent to which some incarcerated serial killers are still quite active orchestrating mayhem and murder. Each enjoys a devout cult following. Take, for example, Charles Manson, a killer who commands dozens of Web pages and was not the least disappointed his parole was recently denied, since he is so busy anyway with computer communications. Manson, of course, is notorious for his ability to get people on the outside to do his bidding, even to attempt assassination of the president. Others, like Richard Ramirez, have whole networks devoted to furthering their Satanic goals. Since the events described in this story were completed, Ramirez continues to press Jason to serve as a lieutenant in his organization.

It is disturbing to discover as well how many famous killers are kings of their prison domain, sitting at the head of a royal court of petitioners, each begging for their time. The coin of the realm is souvenirs. The killers sell their childlike artwork for hundreds of dollars, garnering even more for signed letters. If all you want is access, you still have to pay a fee—pornographic magazine subscriptions, contributions to defense funds, perhaps a little favor or two.

As long as incarcerated killers receive notoriety for their predatory acts, they'll continue to draw lost souls into their kingdoms. For as has been pointed out, people want to get close to things they fear. Fans send "serial killer superstars" not only money but adulation. Women send naked pictures and offers of matrimony. Journalists wait in line for the privilege of conducting an interview. Book and film accounts of killers' lives attract huge audiences. Just like Jason, people want to reach into the darkness without fully understanding the consequences.

In the end, *The Last Victim* is not only the tale of a young man who wandered down a dangerous path and then regained his bearings, it is a parable of what happens in a culture that glorifies violence, denies its fascination, and then makes celebrities out of killers. The message society has come increasingly to accept is that fame is value-neutral. "There can be no bad fame" is the mantra of the airwaves, which is a chilling thought indeed.

JASON MOSS graduated summa cum laude from the University of Nevada, Las Vegas. Since the experiences he recounts in this book, he has served internships with the U.S. Secret Service and the Bureau of Alcohol, Tobacco, and Firearms.

JEFFREY KOTTLER, PH.D., is a practicing psychotherapist and professor of counseling. The author of more than thirty books, he served as Jason's instructor at a UNLV advanced honors seminar.

VISIT US ONLINE @
WWW.TWBOOKMARK.COM

AT THE TIME WARNER BOOKMARK WEB SITE YOU'LL FIND:

- CHAPTER EXCERPTS FROM SELECTED NEW RELEASES

- ORIGINAL AUTHOR AND EDITOR ARTICLES

- AUDIO EXCERPTS

- BESTSELLER NEWS

- ELECTRONIC NEWSLETTERS

- AUTHOR TOUR INFORMATION

- CONTESTS, QUIZZES, AND POLLS

- FUN, QUIRKY RECOMMENDATION CENTER

- PLUS MUCH MORE!

Bookmark Time Warner Trade
Publishing @ www.twbookmark.com